Souvenirs of a Century

An American Original and son
record pop mysteries of modern history

Preface by John Lentilhon

Pictures by Sage Goodwin
Poems by Rufus Goodwin

Afterword: A personal memoir about the painter,
by Rufus Goodwin

Published by Educare Press
PO Box 17222
Seattle, WA 98107

International Standard Book Number: 0-944638-19-8

Library of Congress Cataloging Card Number: 00-190363

Printed in China

10 9 8 7 6 5 4 3 2 1

Book design by Megan Haas

Souvenirs of a Century

Magic Realism
by an American Original and Son

PREFACE

The first Goodwin Senior & Son reached Boston on THE LION in 1630 with John Winthrop, then moved on to Hartford in Connecticut to help found that city. Today's Goodwin Senior, an American Original, now in his nineties, lives on outside the city to this day painting souvenirs of a century.

This is the one reason why surreal icons of the American 19th century mix with the images of the 20th century in the magic realism of Goodwin's paintings. But Goodwin is haunted not just by the Victorian past and the pop culture of this century – he is also fascinated by the future.

"I concoct a skewed vision of time," Goodwin says, "and I paste the past into the present. My images are a warp of culture, but actually I paint things the way I see them." Goodwin sees things others don't, at least relationships — but he makes them visible.

His form of figuration and field composition goes back to the work of

Thomas Hart Benton in this century, an early modernist leader of the new American scene painting with his raw and often violent portrayals of Americana.

But Goodwin's uncle, Phillip Goodwin, was also the first designer of the Museum of Modern Art (MOMA), the man designated by the Rockefellers to appoint his friend Phillip Johnson as the architect for the still extant building; Phil Goodwin was also a friend of Alfred Barr, the legendary first curator of MOMA. It was Johnson's first job and he worked with Phil who was also a collector of the likes of Van Gogh, Klee, and Graves.

Yet Sage Goodwin clung to figuration. His own father's library, where Sage had seen Theodore Roosevelt in person sitting with his dad at the library table, had been chock full of Dickens and Cruikschank, and Goodwin, a draftsman by talent, became a civic architect in Hartford, serving in the Navy Seabees as a Chief Petty Officer in the War, and then designing the Hartford public library.

He retired in 1960 to paint full time. In back of his home in Avon stands the studio Goodwin, where his Oeuvre is housed — about five hundred paintings picturing several centuries of American pop culture. More than eighty pictures have been sold and are in private and public collections around the world.

Goodwin has shown in exhibitions in Paris, New York, Hartford, and New Britain. He has pictures in the permanent collections of the Wadsworth Atheneum and the New Britain Museum of American Art.

He also has two story picture books out in black and white — FAMILY ALBUM, and FUTURE'S FRIENDS.

A limpid poetry of magic realism, conceptually, at least, infuses Goodwin's canvasses with a sometimes haunting, sometimes ominous dislocation of verisimilitude. Often he is whimsical, sometimes downright funny. Some of the pictures in his oeuvre are topical. Even literary. This defies the post-modernist fads of constructionism, minimalism, and installments.

In the best of them an almost musical architectonic composition, in an oil and acrylic palette fairly low-keyed, but decorative, overcomes the visual gag and moves the pictures into a neo-classical timelessness. Goodwin denies having "a vision" but despite himself the pictures, not just ordinary representationalism, are visionary.

His cousin was the painter Kay Sage, a de Chirico style surrealist, married to the French modernist Yves Tanguy. Another cousin was Chick Austin, the curator of the Wadsworth Atheneum who mounted the first show in America 1936 of European surrealism and Dada. Sage Goodwin went to the famous Hartford costume ball of that year that inaugurated the show destined to influence one line of American art almost as much as the New York Armory show of 1913.

Goodwin is no Grandpa Moses. He is not a naïve painter. He did not enter the fray, although self-taught, completely untutored.

Often Goodwin works from newspaper and magazine imagery, pasting and drawing collages with ink washes as cartoons for the final pictures. His voracious historical and cultural reading informs the literary references of his paintings.

Goodwin's service to American art is twofold. He stuck by the early modernist figuration of Benton, Burchfield, and the Ashcan school despite the throes of abstraction, minimalism, and conceptualism. Goodwin's view is that what goes around comes around, and that the values of yesterday and tomorrow — a major artist like Benton that goes into decline — come back in fads and cycles. Goodwin's work today qualifies in its eclectic ethos as genuinely post-modern.

His second contribution to American art is an almost entirely original promotion of the historicity and primacy of American pop icons, from Victorian boats and dresses to neo-classical houses and horse and carriages into the ultra modern culture of cars and comics, making an amalgam of time past, present, and future into a kind of legendary, mythological and timeless snapshot of America.

In this, Goodwin breaks definitely with the European tradition, and the academic painting, but nor does he follow the facile gallery fusionism or avantgardism of media culture. He remains his own man.

The 21st century may look on Goodwin's work not from the point of view of Picasso and Matisse's aestheticism, nor from the non-objective point of view of Jackson Pollock and Mark Rothko, or even from the pop hard-line realism of Warhol, but as a body of post-modern figuration and conceptual "magic" realism spanning a century and forging a symbiotic imagery for its pop disparities in soft line.

I could have wished, in this undertaking, that Goodwin had been a bit more painterly, ala Balthus, referencing his palate and chromaticism a little more lingeringly, tasting his oils, and certainly tending to more underpainting and higher finish. Unlike many magic realists, however, he did overcome his considerable talent for drawing and let the brush depict the detail.

He did also understand that he was an artist of commitment, fashion and iconography and a vehicle, not just a Sunday painter. Despite his denials, he revered the studio and the mission of the artist in transforming reality. He did it with a mixture of skepticism and panache, a combination of cynicism and wonder.

SMALL HOUSE OWNER is an acute en plein air study of the real unseen
American psyche, a pictorial gem for the gallery and a unique exercise in
the classicism of low culture as yet unseen in any of the canonical schools
of even American academicians, while THE HOUSE NEXT DOOR tells
of the passing of an era and passage of an American way of life.

The poetry of his son narrates these images an internal landscape that
complements the pictures — lighting up the lyric impression of the
iconography, much like a commentator on an illuminated manuscript.
This is the art of the poem as caption. Together the poems and pictures
are time capsules of a century and the Millennium.

In an age of TV bites and cyberspace, the Goodwins, Senior & Son, are
content providers — their freight is not the canons of old or even of
modernism, but of the culture itself, and they provide an outsider's eye
and ear to move forward.

John Lentilhon
Curator for studio Goodwin

SOUVENIRS OF A CENTURY

ONE

HOUSE NEXT DOOR

That house haunts me, and I haunt
The house, though I am not yet dead,
Yet I am a memory in my father's house
As father's house is memory in me.
The cypress yearns for afterlife,
As all we who are born yearn;
The path home leads into the past
As a spirit of Greece still remembers us.
Here, here a poem walks up to the present,
Up to the home that is now a memory.
We all will be homeless in some future
Even as the sea itself rises and washes
Away the coasts, and an era will become
Like old architecture on the green grass.

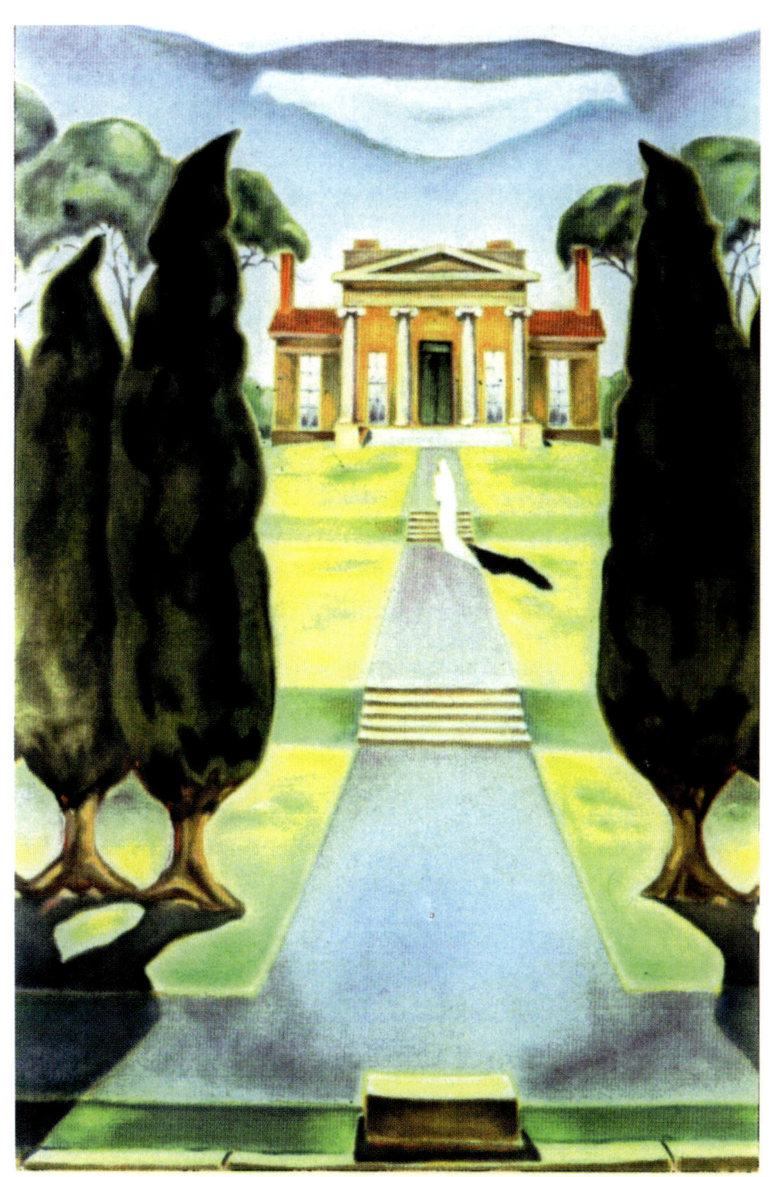

The House Next Door 30" x 40"

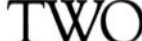

PRAIRIE FLOWER

She looked out upon a vision,
But the vision was her mirror self;
It was the grand industrial park
Dreaming of her that led to a nation.
The prairie dust turned into coal.
The prairie grass turned into oil
The prairie fire turned into gas.
Gone was the prairie flower, the girl
Who had truly become woman at last.
What future would she dream of last night?
What did tonight dream of her?
She was the future staring at the plains,
She bore the coming life of tomorrow.
She was tomorrow about to be kissed
Leaning on the surroundings that bury us.
Hers are the prairie lips and the cool
Look that turned the river to glass.

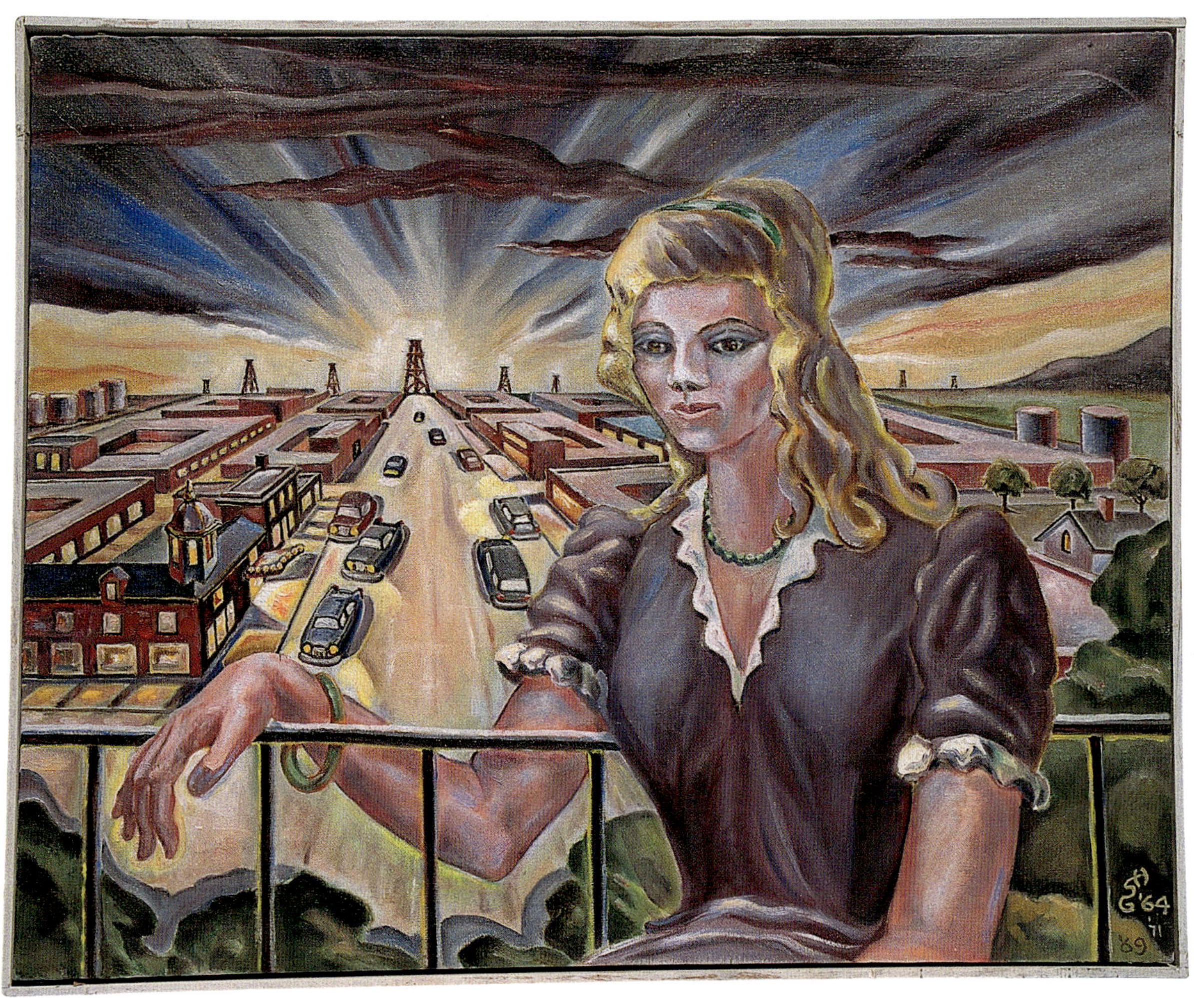

Prairie Flower   28" x 22"

THREE

SUNSET BOULEVARD

Fay is her name; they name her
A street; it is down at the crossroads
Where one day she hopes she will meet
The man of her dreams at the junction,
The man with the golden feet.
It will be at the famous corner
Of Sunset Boulevard and Fay
Where pretty face and an undressed body
Meet the directors, and the candid cameras play.
All she has to hide is a scar.
Ahead it says, "Stop", but Fay
Will head on, right by the telephone pole
Like a cross. Yes, ahead it says, "Stop",
At the crossroads of loss.

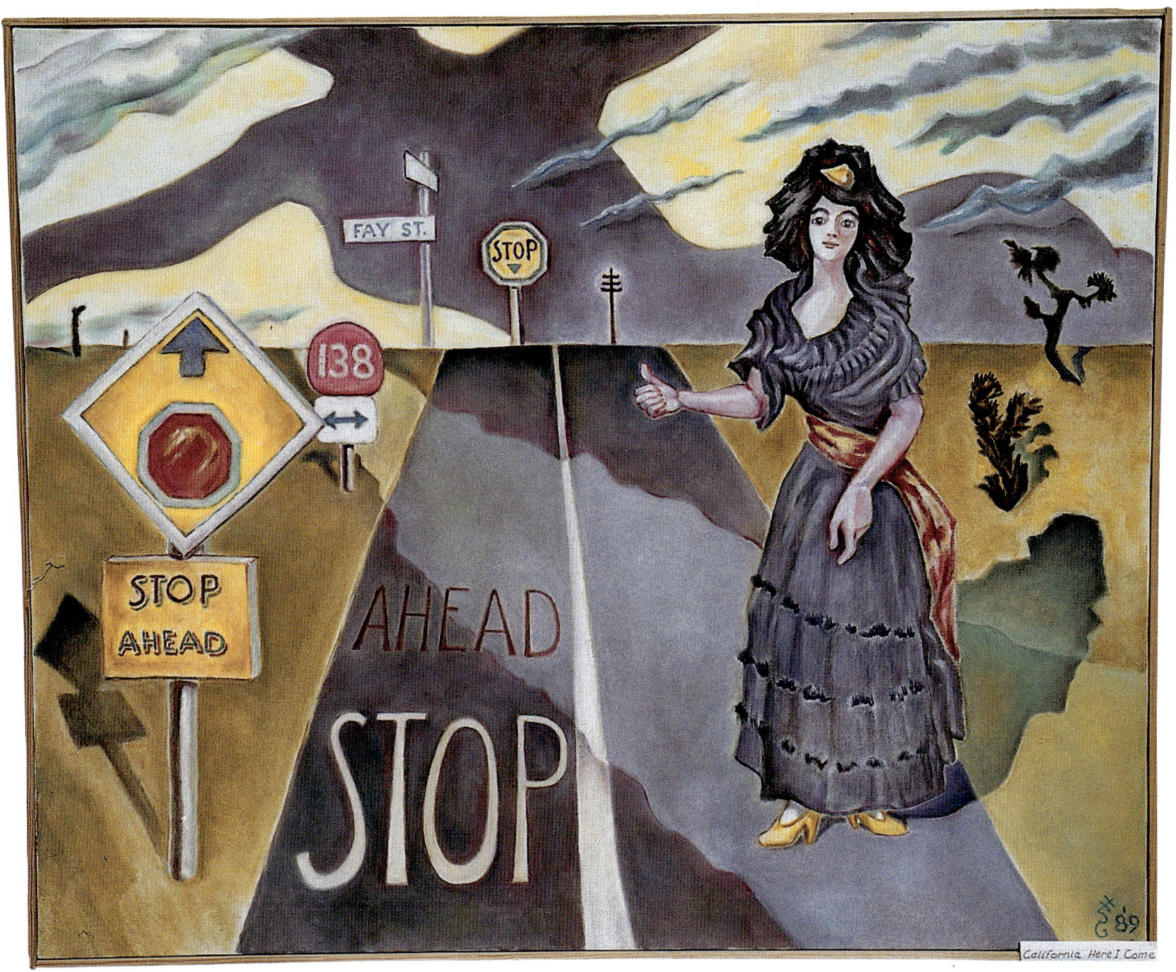

SUNSET BOULEVARD 35" x 28"

FOUR

MARCHING CARDS

Jack of Diamonds is the real guy,
Mr. Lover on the steps, a jewel
In his pocket, but I am the Three of Spades
Who has just mowed Daddy's lawn.
The cards have all been expelled
From the stone manse to go marching.
To the money or even lament.
Needles of the Lebanese cedar
Wave above the leaping green garden,
The Greek vase gathers the cold waters
And the Ace of Hearts is ultimate charge.
Down the marble steps the maiden awaits
And an unpainted fountain splashes
Water that rushes from under the stone throne.

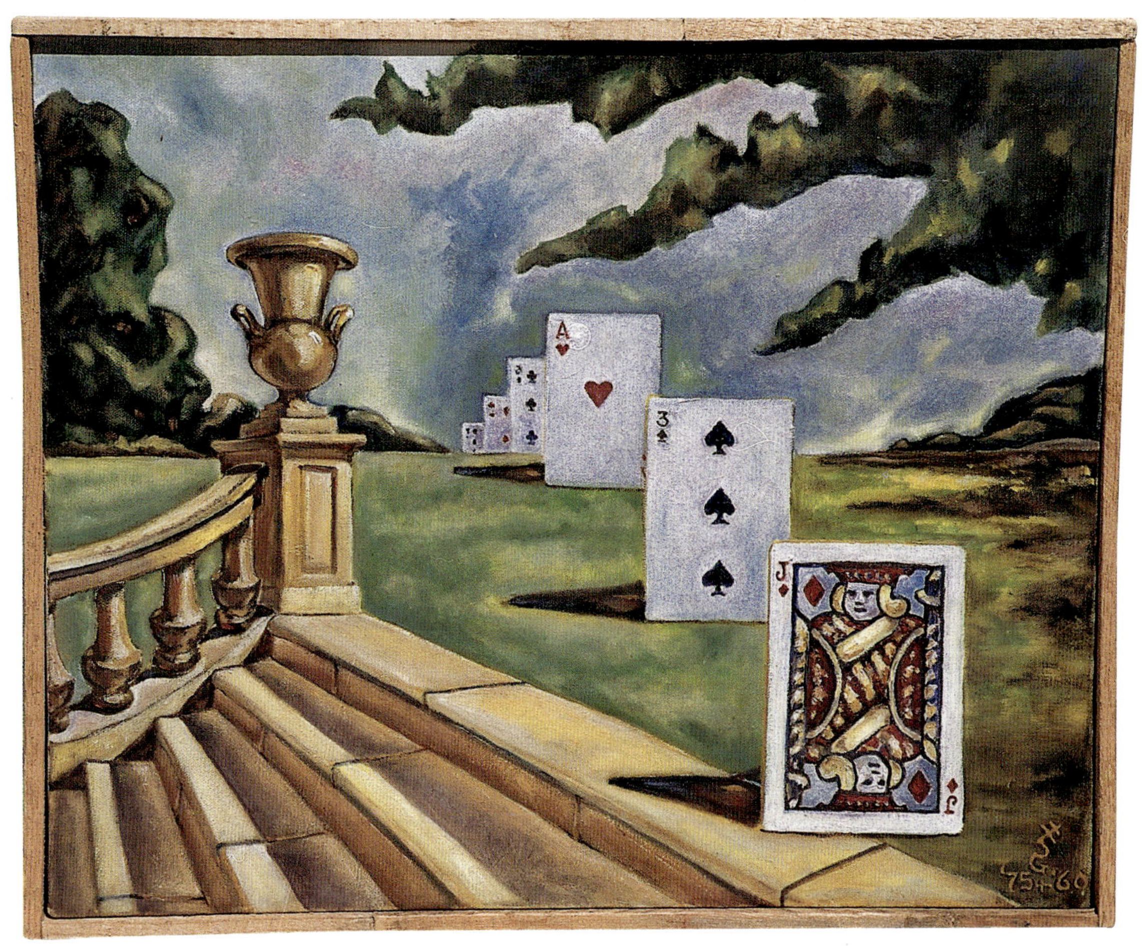

MARCHING CARDS   20" x 16"

FIVE

WHITE HORSE IN AUTUMN

I am the old man in the end
Coming towards myself out of the past,
The driver of a coach coming to take me,
The last of a turning century.
The horse is a dead ember of the road.
Trees are barren for an acornless winter.
The dark coach rolls like a hearse.
This road comes from far off memory
That goes shortly not into the distance
But into us in the very present
Where we the viewer look on at Time.
There is no noise in the hanging leaves,
No music in the groves to right or left.
Omniscient the face of my coachman peers
Into us like a destination ahead
That is us, like the night, like the night.

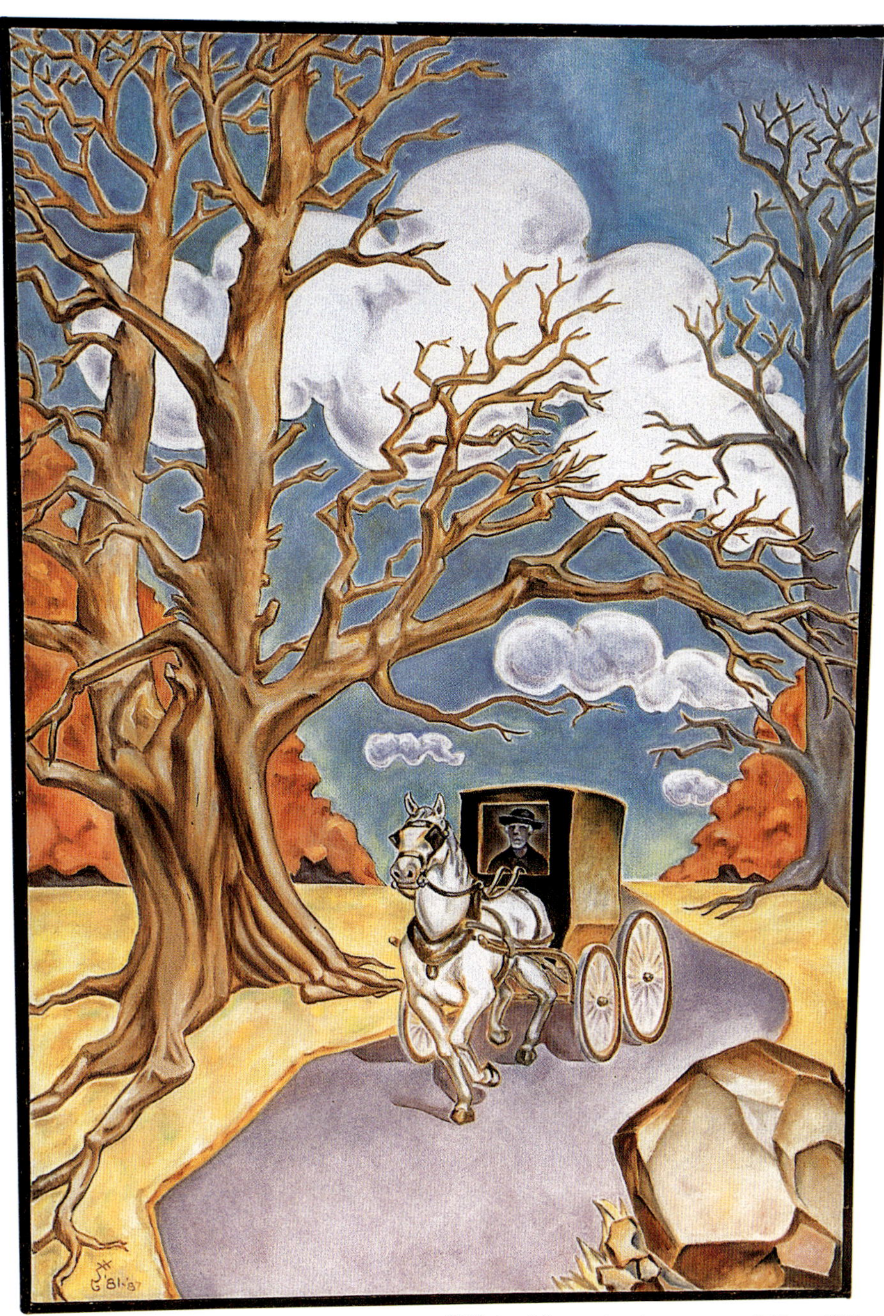

White Horse in Autumn   34" x 50"

SIX

PORPHYRY COLUMN

I am become old man Apollo
On the roof, ancient voyeur,
Have plucked my hollow stone lyre
And shadow is my only echo,
Shadow behind the porphyry column.
Golden hair throws no shadow
But is the pure air of my music
Which stares into the unseen viewer,
 The lover looking at her picture.
Music is the last mover of motion
While around the corner, ruins,
And the temple in a sunken ocean.

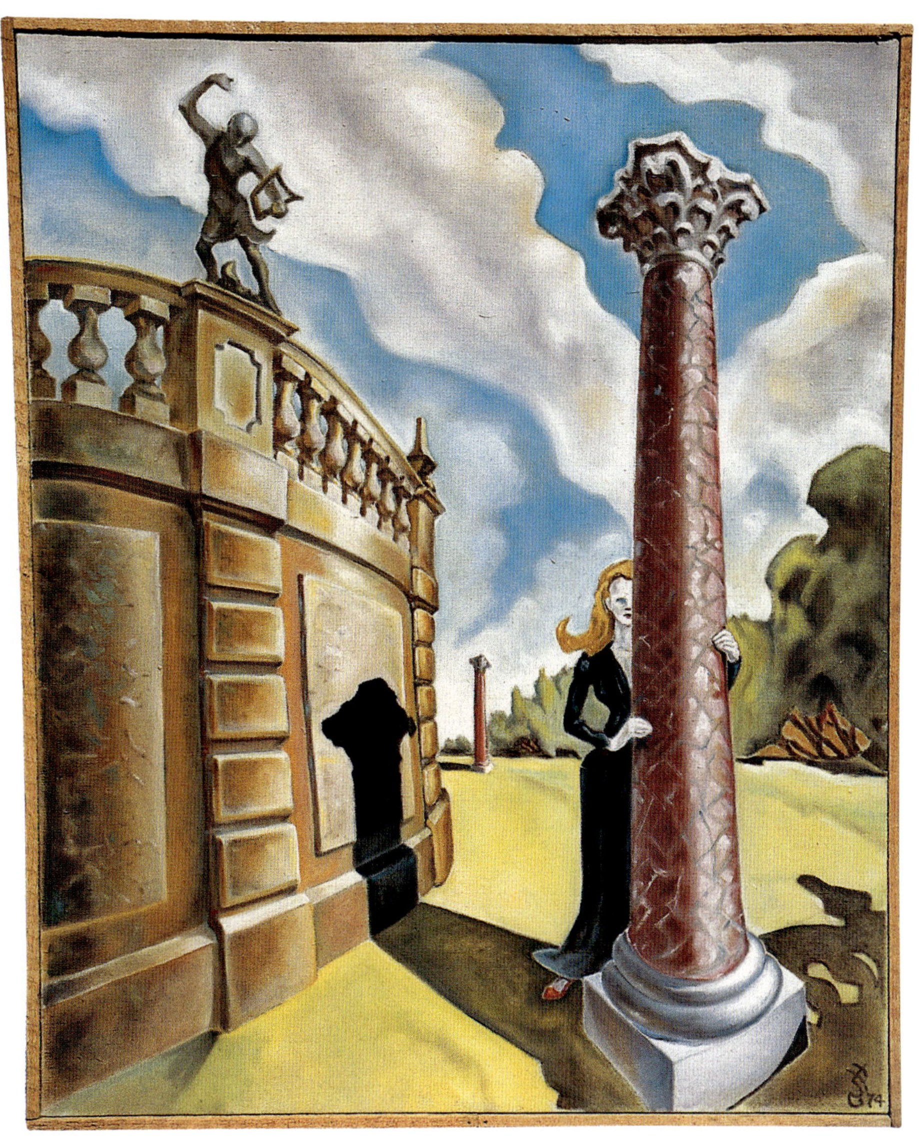

Porphyry Column   27" x 33"

SEVEN

REUNION IN SPRING

At Grandfather's red brick mansion,
Memory plays its usual trick,
And ghostlike he is standing
Greeting Time, the old witch.
He is the gallant sometime Confederacy,
And she is the youth of the North,
And across a bed of Spring tulips
He says, "I loved you so much."
He says it with his hat doffed,
And she leans on her cane. "I cannot
today," She repeats with her grim grin,
"For soon, oh so soon, it will rain."
A century forgets them, the cherry tree,
And the house now, my dear, is quite empty.

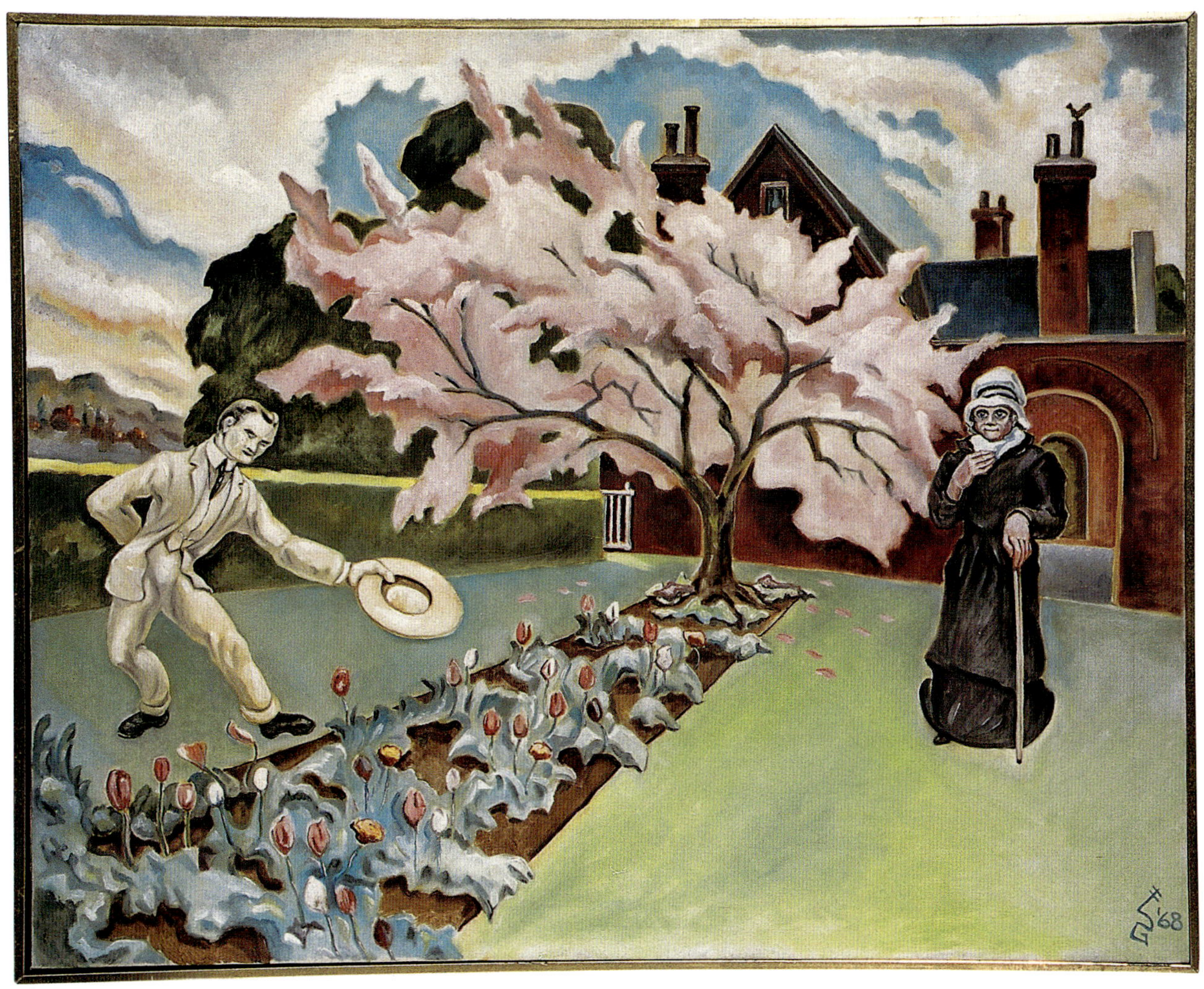

Reunion In Spring   36" x 28"

EIGHT

FLIGHT

Except for the poem I am the empty man
Sitting vacant in the shelter entry,
The man without an idea in his cup of coffee.
The man under a box in the corner lot.
Without words, I am an empty cipher,
A face without features in God's movie,
A mute puppet of anonymous life,
A lost eye. A lost leg. An empty hand
Held outward for spare change. Without the poem
My clothes are rags, my soul a vacuous
Passing puff on a butt end of a day.
The poems is only the pursuit of meaning
Even onto the gutter, Sitting by a drain,
Watching the drenching rain splutter down.
And the newspaper like a scrap of moment
Float toward the ever coming of evening.
Give me your hand, O evening star,
And light me over the homeless night.
Give me your arm, O pain, O poem
And hold my hand in never ending Big City.
Except for the poem I am a dead man
Walking like a truck toward dawn;
Without the poem I am without shelter
And cannot talk to my winged angel,
The homeless angel thrown out of heaven
That stretches to the end of the city
Like the street. Except for the poem
I have none of the world's endless money;
Except for the poem I have nothing to eat.
Without the poem I have no one to love.

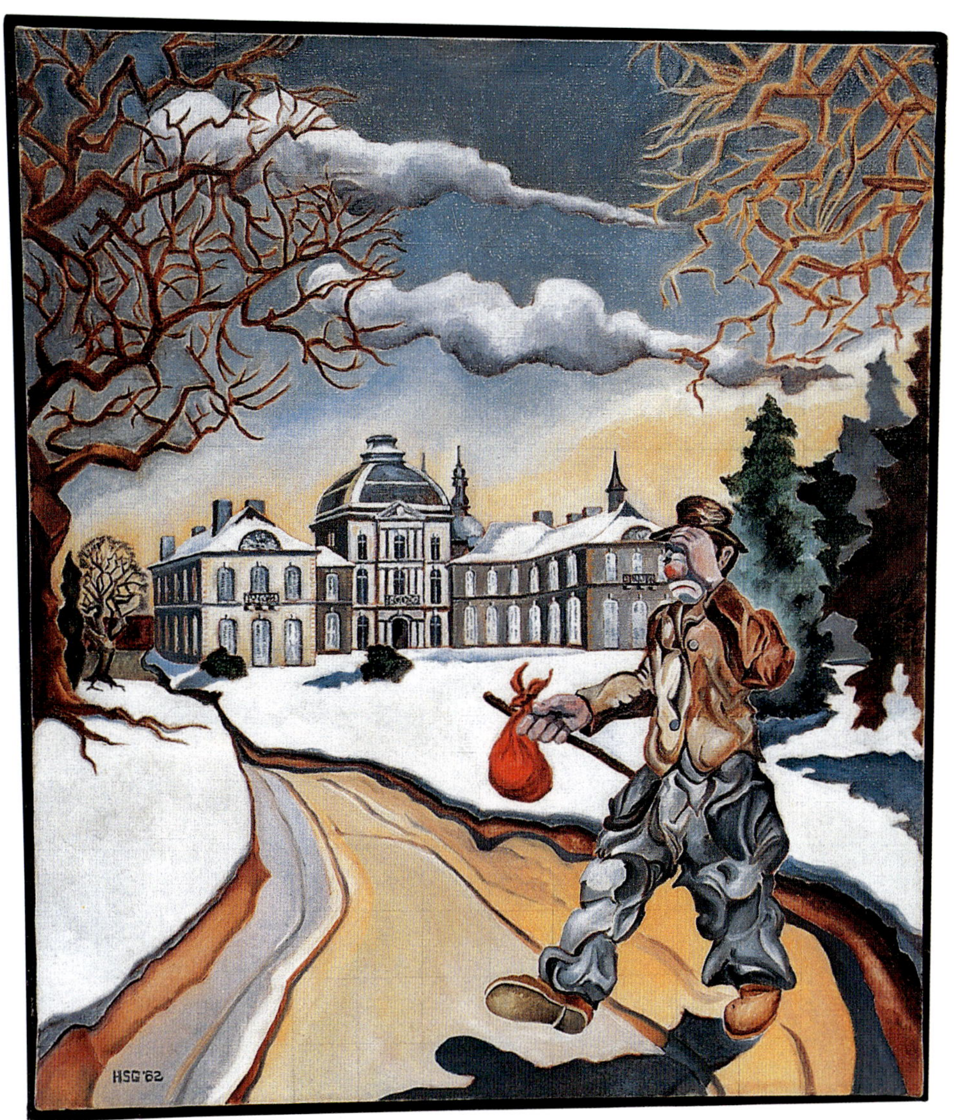

Flight   28" x 32"

NINE

RIVER BOAT

Sailing toward the dollar bill
Yesteryear's steamboat heads West
Where the bank stands in the sunset
Full of our ancient green cash.
The new river flows from back East
And Greek columns of the family house
Are fading into the vessel's wake
While up ahead the future looms large.
The gray cloud is the elegiac note
In the trouble sky of the mind,
And the old man's time is a forgotten painting,
Virtual reality of oil and acrylic,
Images which might one day surface with a click
On the inevitable blue Internet
Like a painted landscape on a silver screen.

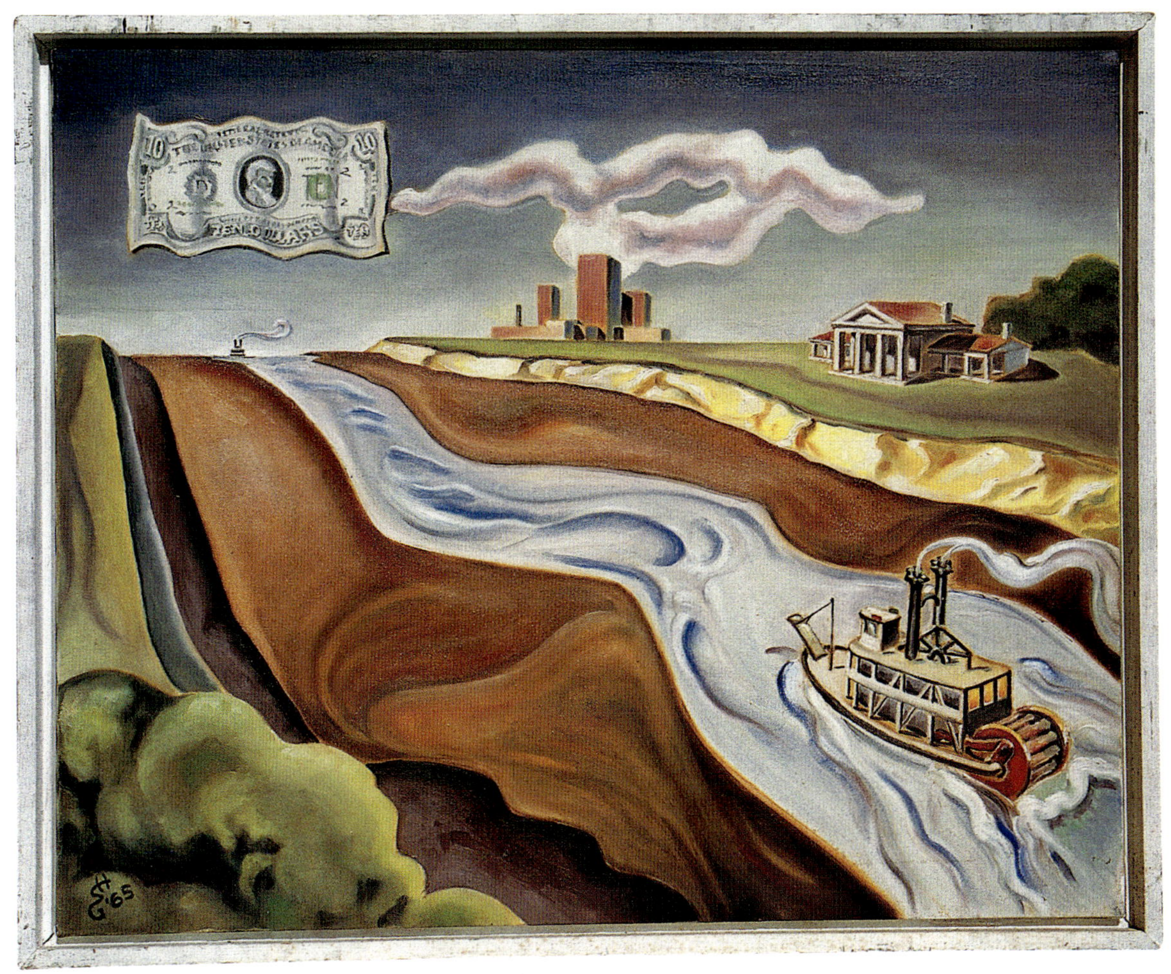

River Boat   28" x 22"

TEN

BUTTERFLY AND CATERPILLAR

In the new age of electronics
The voyeur clicks a vision;
No one any longer knows where beauty
Went in, where the fairy tale ended.
Even the devil can no longer stare
At his lover without goggles on.
Even she covers her hooded eyes.
His is a mere kind of cyber love,
No flower blooms, no music;
There are no sweet words to say anymore.
In fact, they both look on at us
In a kind of decimated horror,
For we are the passing picture,
The gallery, where now the painting
Of them looks at us on the wall.

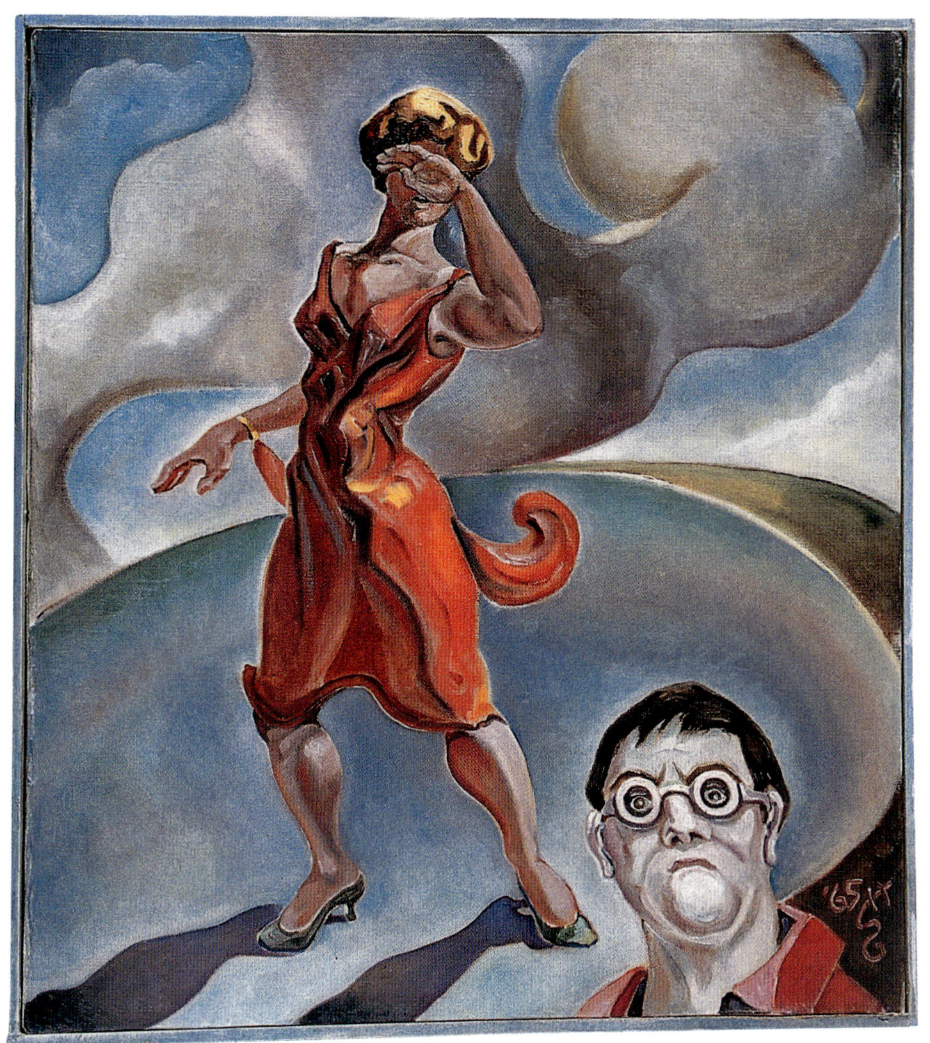

Butterfly and Caterpillar   20" x 22"

ELEVEN

CARD GAME

I would bet on the orange blond
A few dollars in shiny silver
Because Bert, the black bar tender,
Might bring me the luck of the night.
For I have wandered into an old Western
In Salt Bend, into a card game
That has lasted a whole century.
Always the dealer held a full house.
It is a house full of memories
From the saloon of the brass past
And to pocket a few thoughts for the future
Is all we can do with chance.

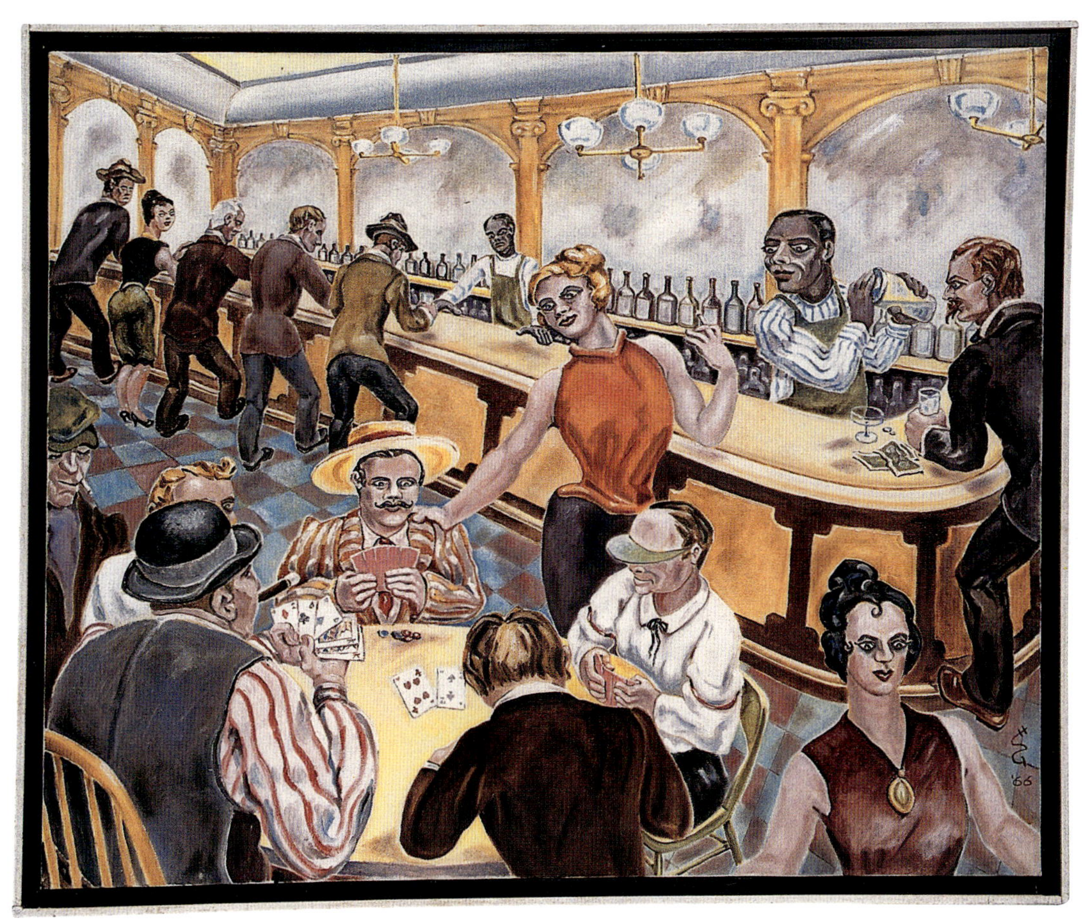

CARD GAME 30" x 24"

TWELVE

EXECUTIVE DAYDREAM

That woman is dreaming of me again,
I can tell, because my mind
Responds like a busy telephone
To her very incandescence of thought.
In fact, I am a thought in her brain,
And from my office I look out
Into her inevitable invitation,
The boat of Sunday headed to sea,
Beyond the lighthouse of land,
Towards the very ocean of dreams
And I write on the window of love,
"Yours truly," till the buzzer rings.

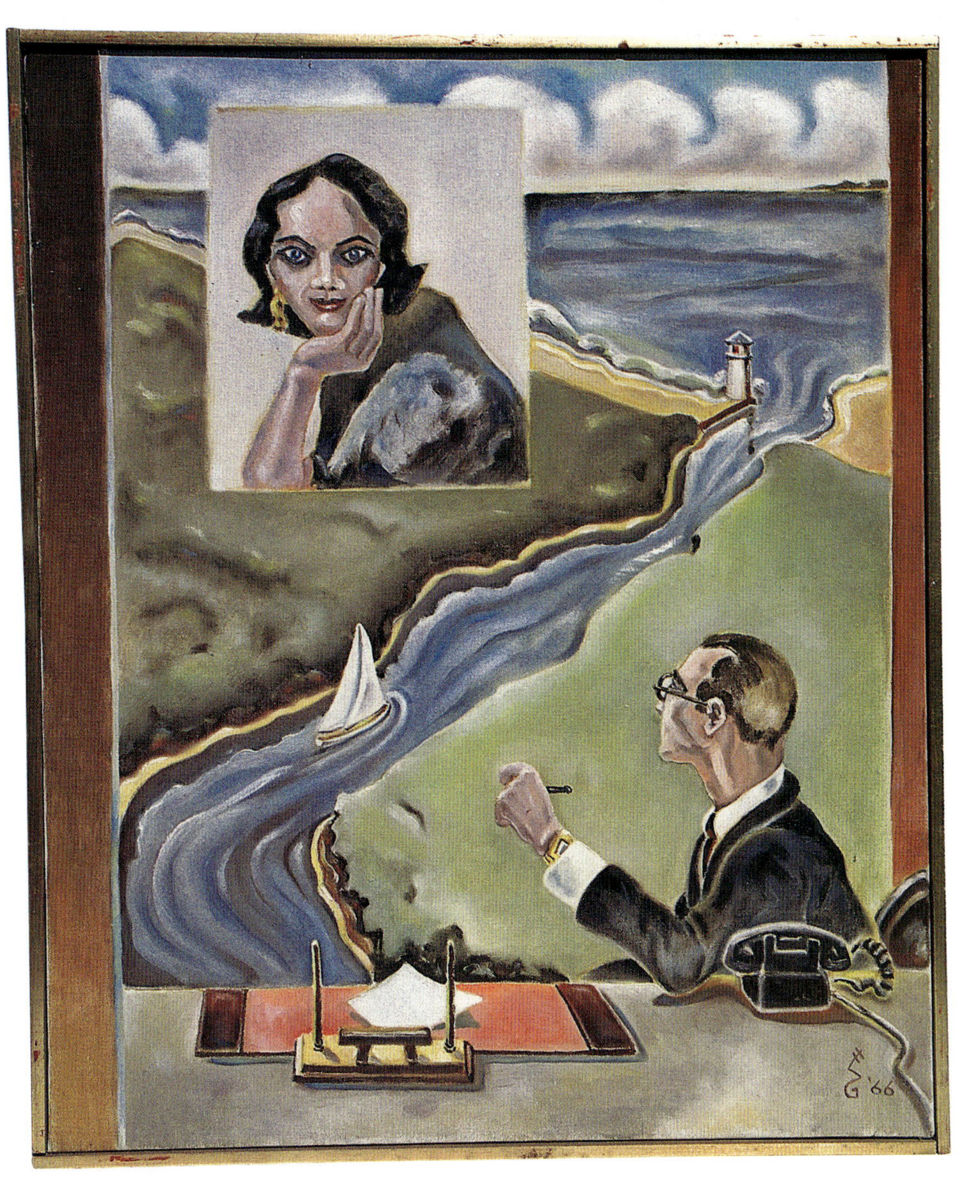

EXECUTIVE DAYDREAM 20" x 24"

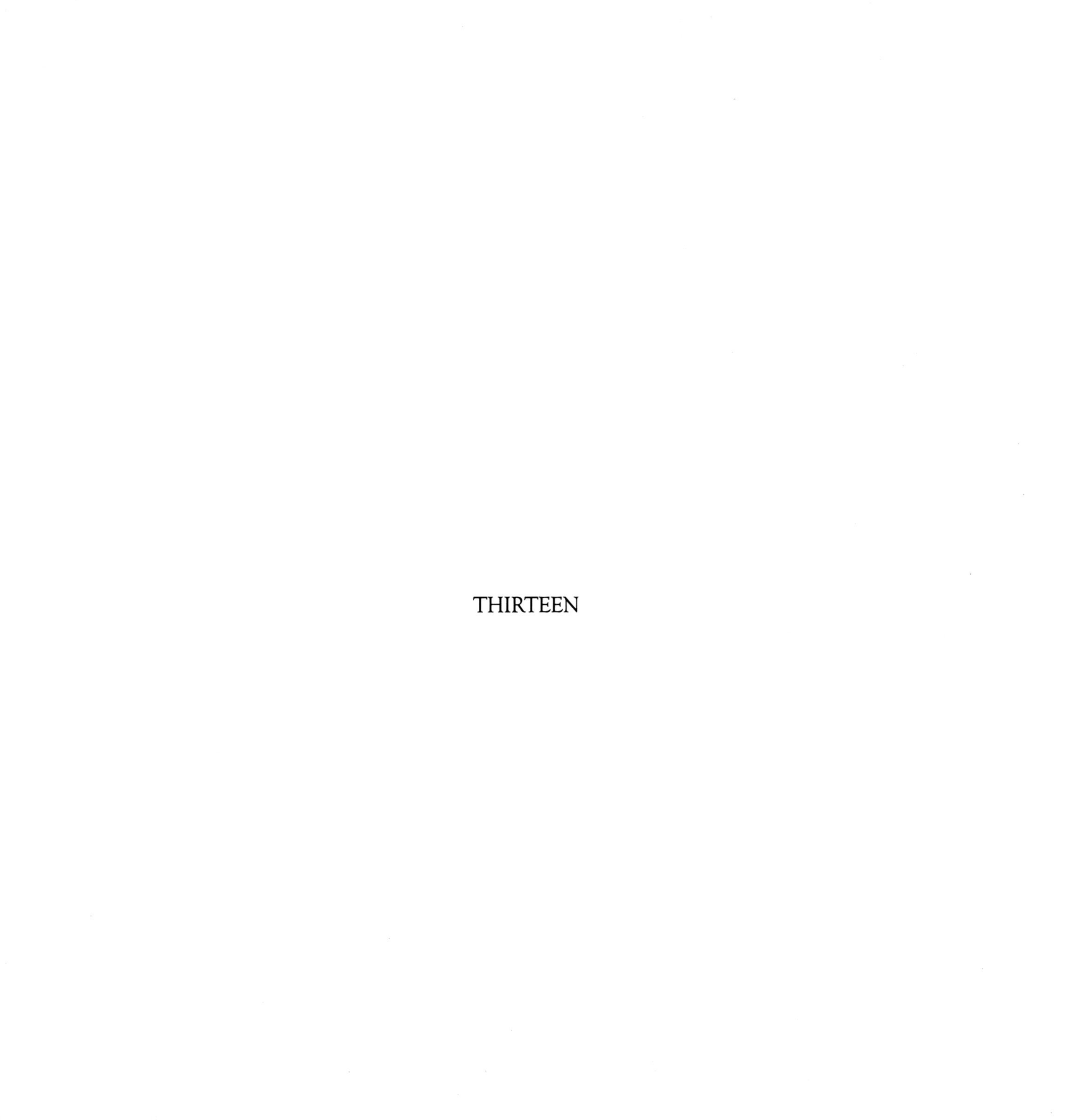

THIRTEEN

TOWN & COUNTRY

Each soul has at least two selves
Under the pine cones, by the lake,
As it dreams of its own identity.
Each dream is a young girl,
Each young girl is a cocoon.
City girl is closeted in a concept
Like a coffin, a town apartment
Where ideas are all rectangular.
Country girl dreams of town too,
But her freedom is like a tree
Rooted in the soil. Her hair is wild.
For her freedom is a dream within.
The girl from town is free from outside
But her life is all groomed and permed.
Her hair, unlike leaves, is citified.

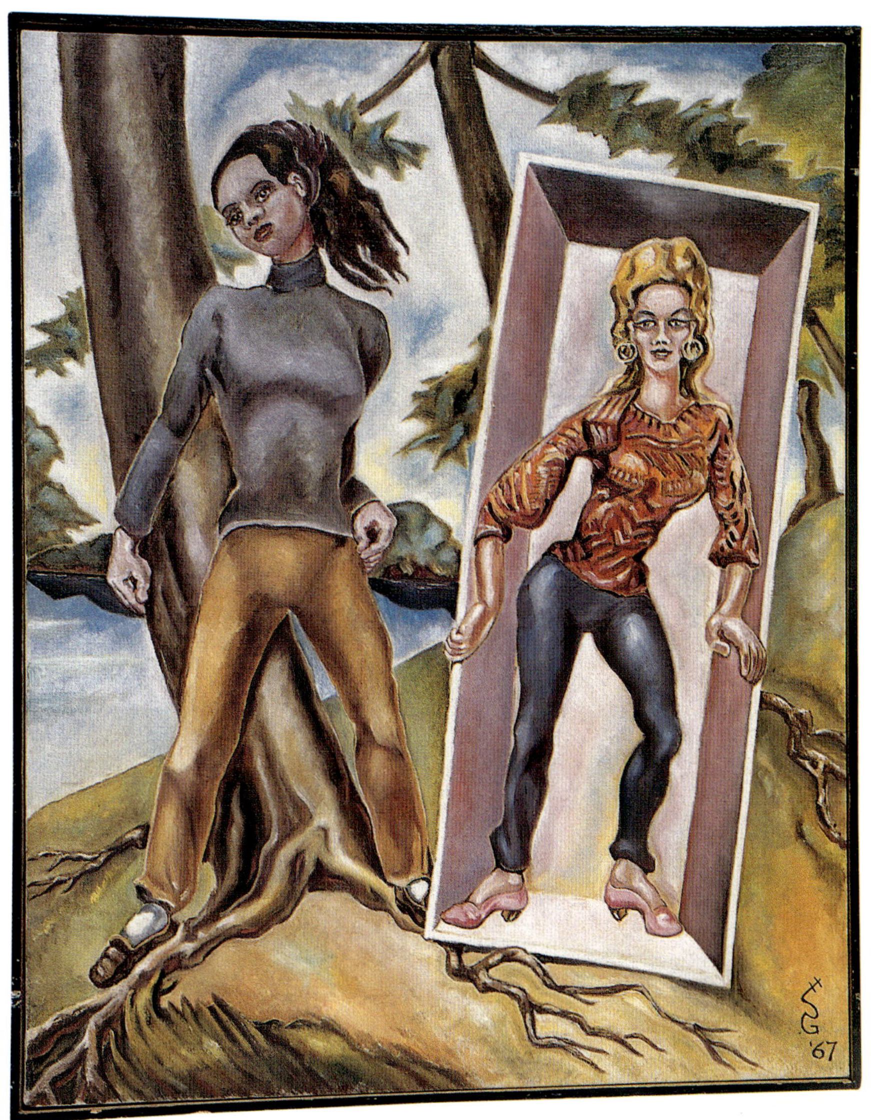

TOWN and Country 24" x 30"

FOURTEEN

INDIAN SCOUT

The Indian of old still rides,
His horse is now the ghost of our soul.
Yes, the scout performs in the rodeo,
And the old culture still gallops about.
But he is looking into a far future
That we cannot see, because we
Are in cars and have killed the instinct.
We spend our lives on the road,
We have paved over the past.
The Indian sees. The India knows.
The lost world of his was majestic.
He sees where yesterday could have lead
But we have driven over our own intentions.

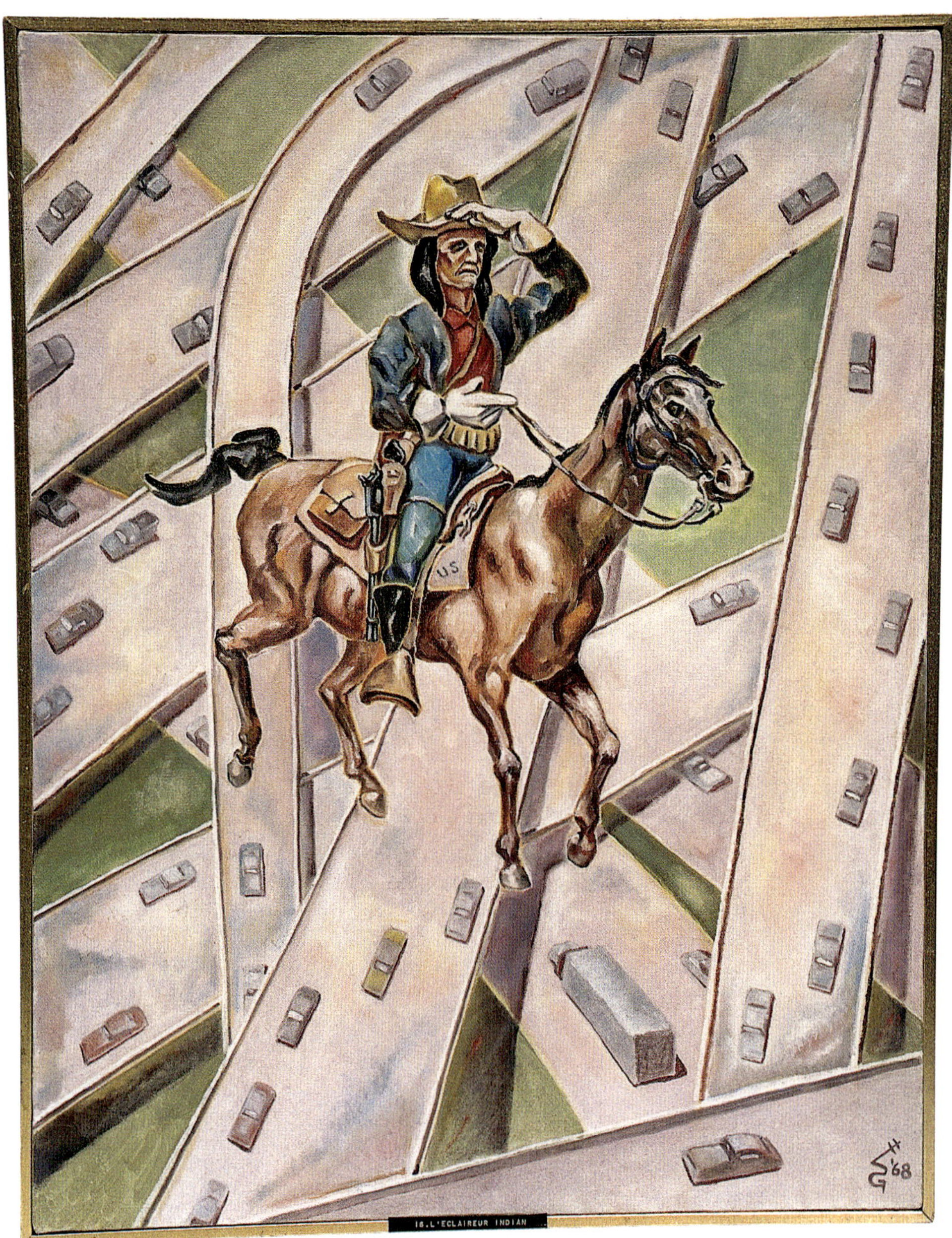

Indian Scout 22" x 28"

FIFTEEN

SMALL HOMEOWNER

On his private American lawn, Br. Butch
Did not even converse with himself,
No, he spoke to exactly nobody
On his pension (wholly himself had earned),
And owed, yes, owed exactly nobody
For his lawn, which he also exactly had earned,
And sat on like the kind of this world
With his palace zoned into place,
A kind of eminent domain unto himself,
Mr. Butch, whom nobody could tell
Ever to go away, but he could tell
Them a thing or two, he could,
Even down to what Mrs. Butch
Would have said (who was already dead),
So Mr. Butch was married to TV,
Dude of the front door and green grass,
Did not even converse with himself,
No, he spoke to exactly nobody.

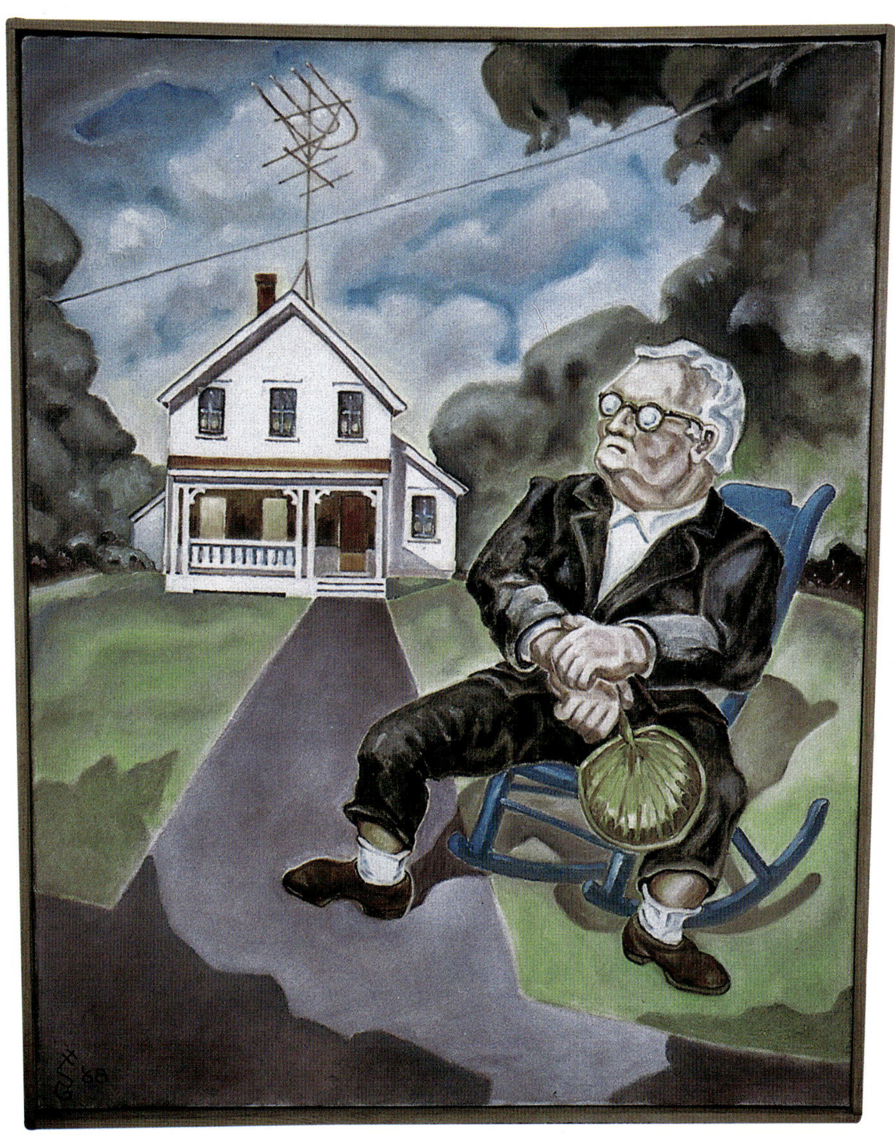

Small Homeowner 16" x 24"

SIXTEEN

THREE QUARTER TIME

There goes the man in the haunted tux,
Black caparisoned, bow tie,
Is he somehow down on his damned luck,
Or has someone told him an awful lie?
He walks bare foot across the beach
In long tails — who is this solitary,
The tall loner in the satin tux?
High silk hat, the dark cylinder,
Vanishes downtide like a silhouette;
He danced tonight with lovely Belinda,
But has no socks on; his cuffs are wet.
Who is the long man in the long tails
Vanishing across the bright sand;
Moonlight wraps him in deep regret
But we don't know half the whole truth yet.
What is that in his right hand,
A glove or a knife? Or a white slipper?
Down down down on his velvet luck,
He seems to be looking still for Belinda,
Wearing his tall tall black cylinder,
Is he looking for the face of a drowned gowned wife
Or just for himself lost in this life?

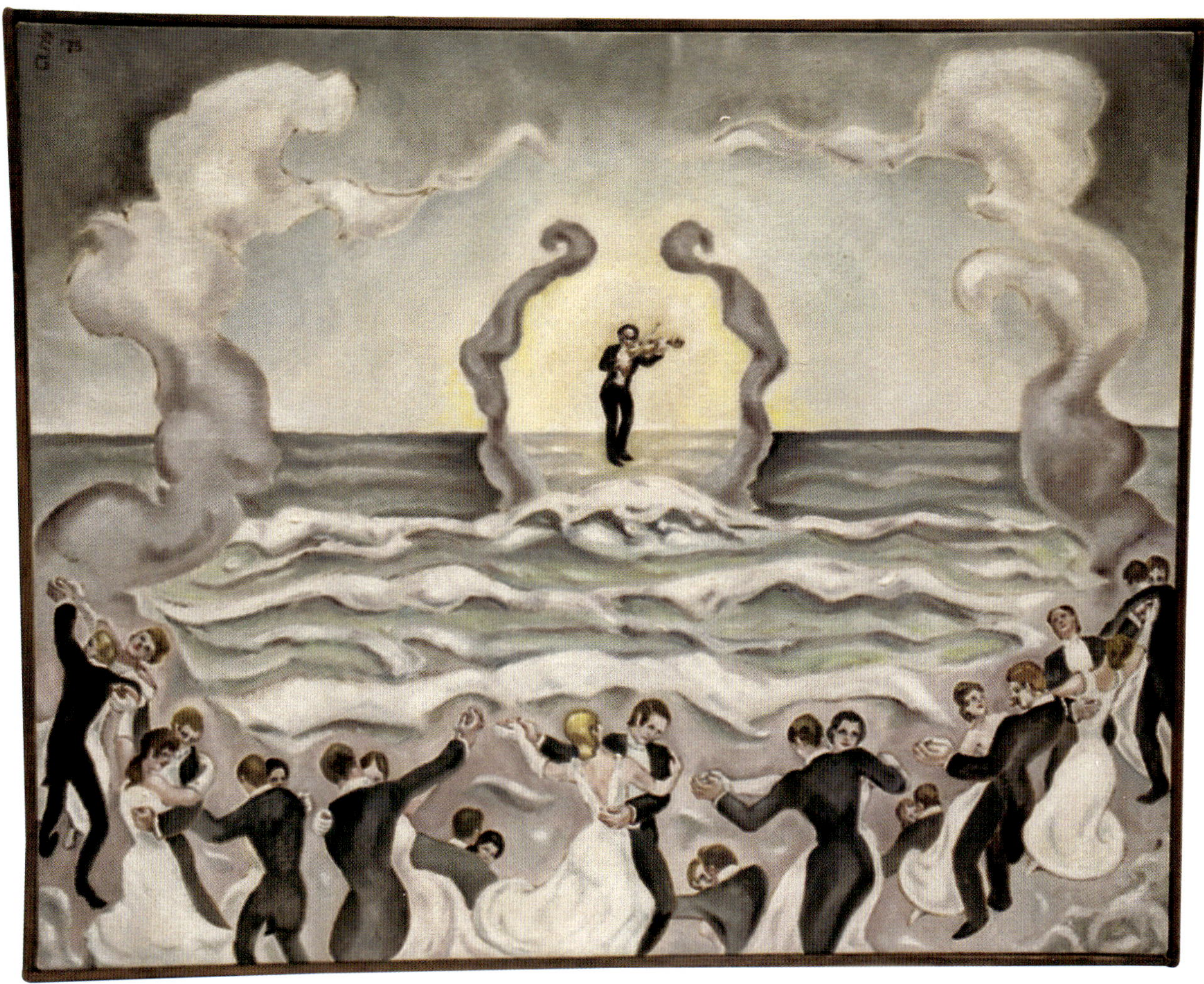

Three Quarter Time 28" x 22"

SEVENTEEN

TWILIGHT

Man is back from the moon
From his voyage into empty heaven,
And having made the cosmos smaller
Now he is sorry by the ancient shore.
He weeps for the once virgin moon,
For the heaven of real wings and angels,
By the sound of prayer and murmuring sea.
Now moon is just another pebble in the sky
But the real world is at his feet,
These stones of this earth unexplored.
This world of the heart is closer
Than the great abstractions of space,
And a moon in the sky is nearer than
Lifeless rocks in a weightless suit.
The real man who steps out of his car,
This man who is here can explore his own life
Or watch for an omen of shooting star.

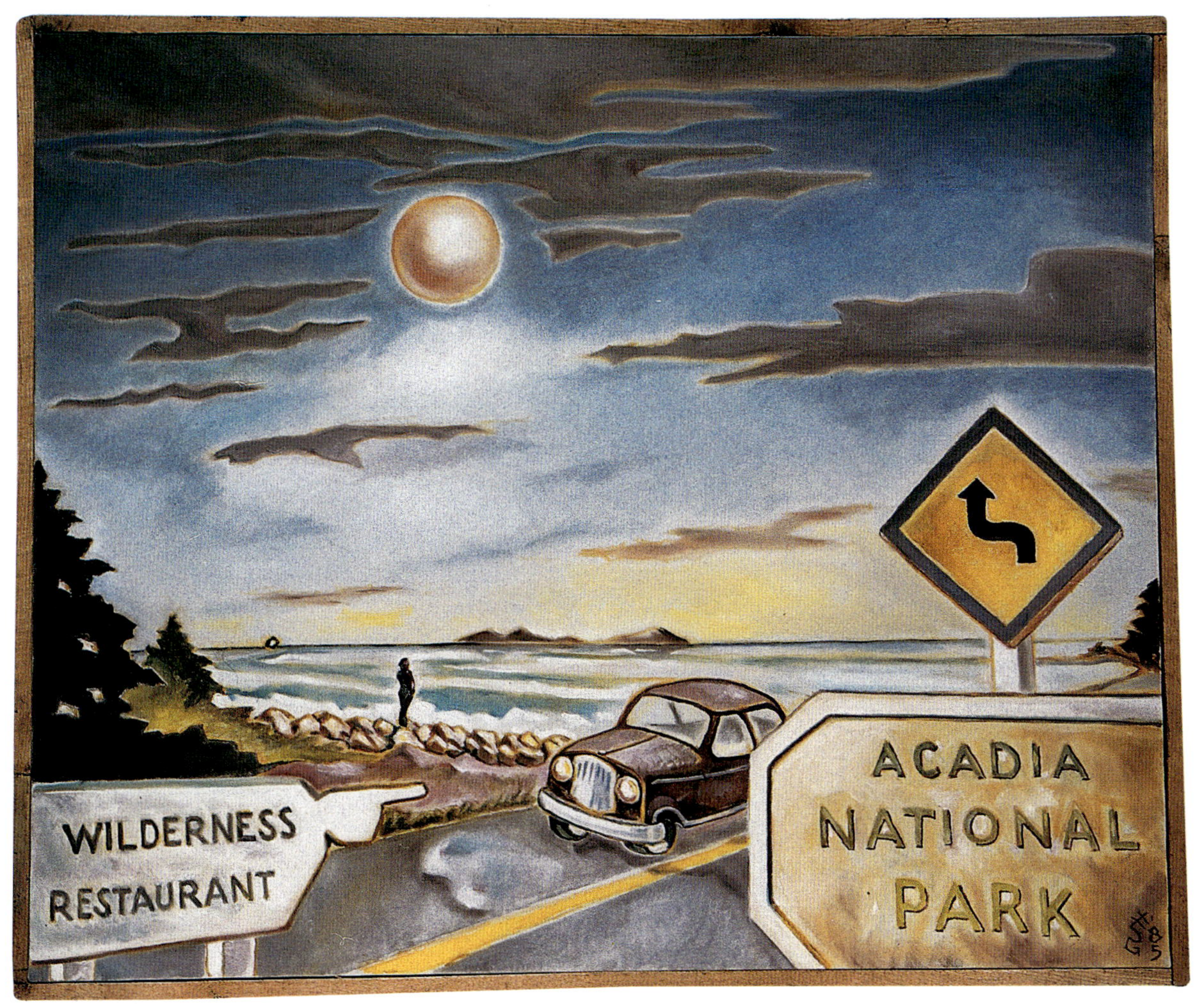

Twilight 30" x 24"

EIGHTEEN

LIGHTHOUSE

The nude dreams of the lighthouse
Are a beacon for her love life,
Love life the island of our soul
On the ocean of the inner eye.
She is sun bathing in the sunset,
While the waves lap at her mind,
Remembering the future of life
Like a crustacean without shell.
Her hair flows like the very water,
The wind whispers a sandy song,
The fishes of paradise swim unseen.
In the air hers is a pregnant thought
That brings a poem to birth like trees,
And her lover is the unseen God
Who built this lone island in the lee.

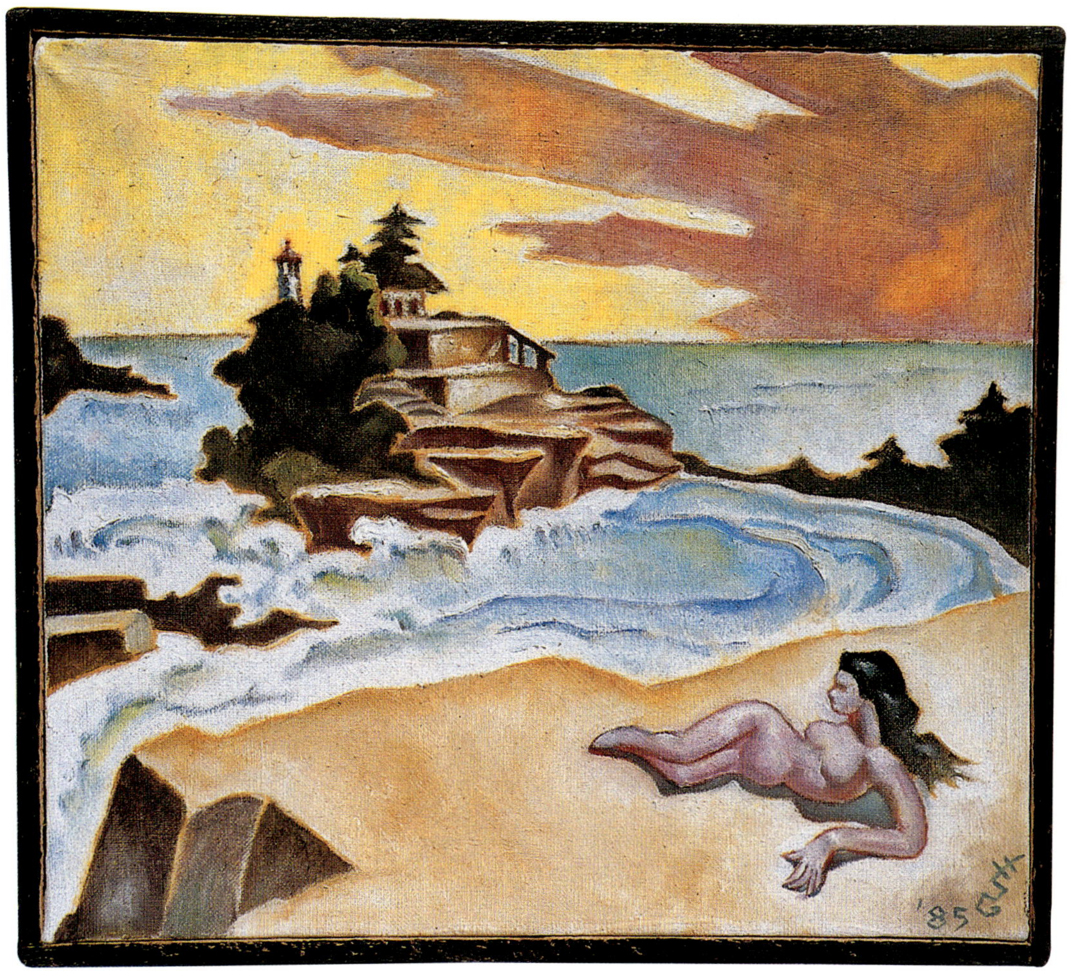

The Lighthouse 15" x 13"

NINETEEN

HOUSE WITH OVAL WINDOWS

The lagoon laps in the lee memory
Of home and other many leavetakings;
The sailor is returned from his dream
And gleaming day on sparkling waters.
His hand holds firm the tiller of life
Because he is steering his own existence
Back to the house with oval windows
Where wife and her eyes still greets him.
It has been a long voyage, this Sunday,
All through the events of the years,
But the boat steers with a soft wind
And the man is master of his own sails.
This should be the same vessel to bear
His bones in the ultimate year to come;
He should drink last wine on the Sound
While the coastal train passes him by.

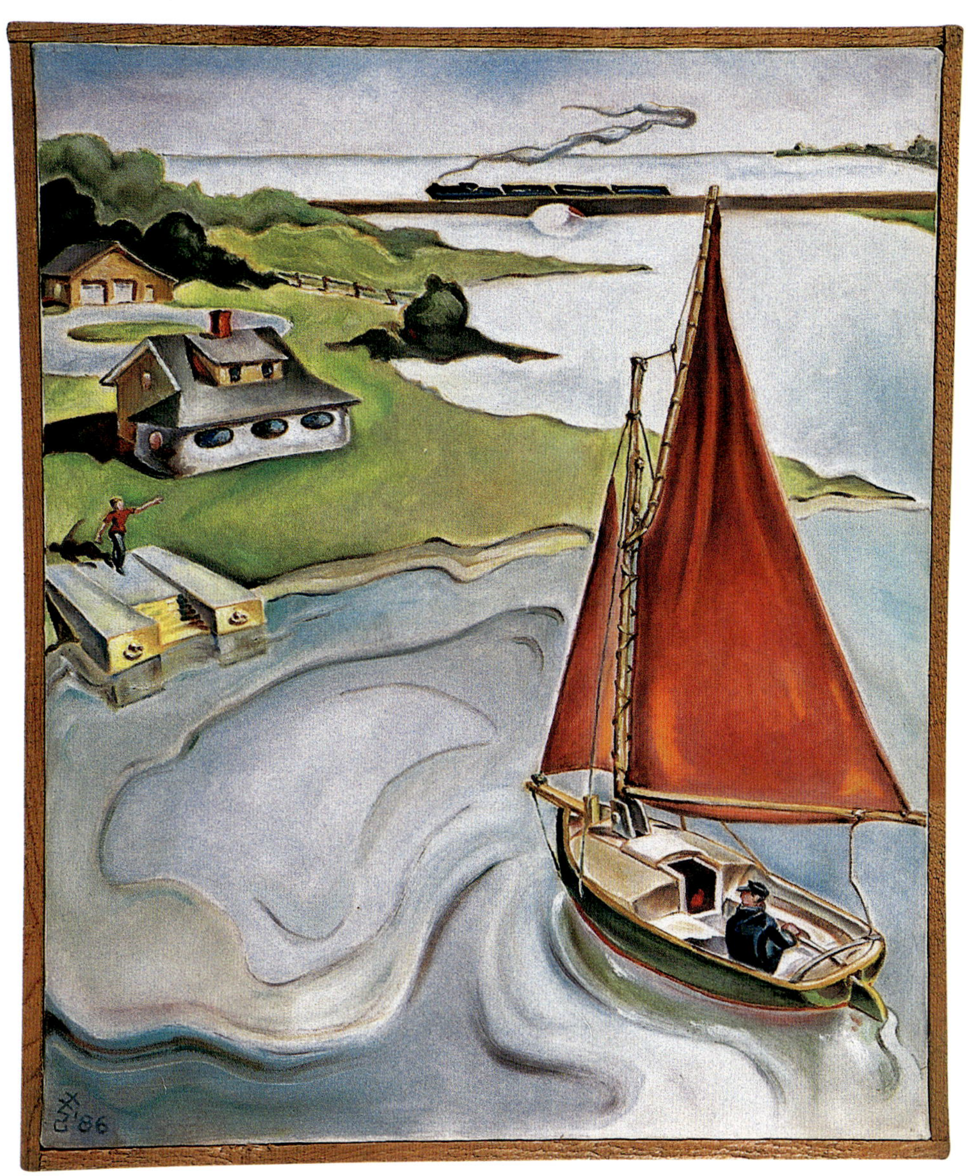

House with Oval Windows 30" x 24"

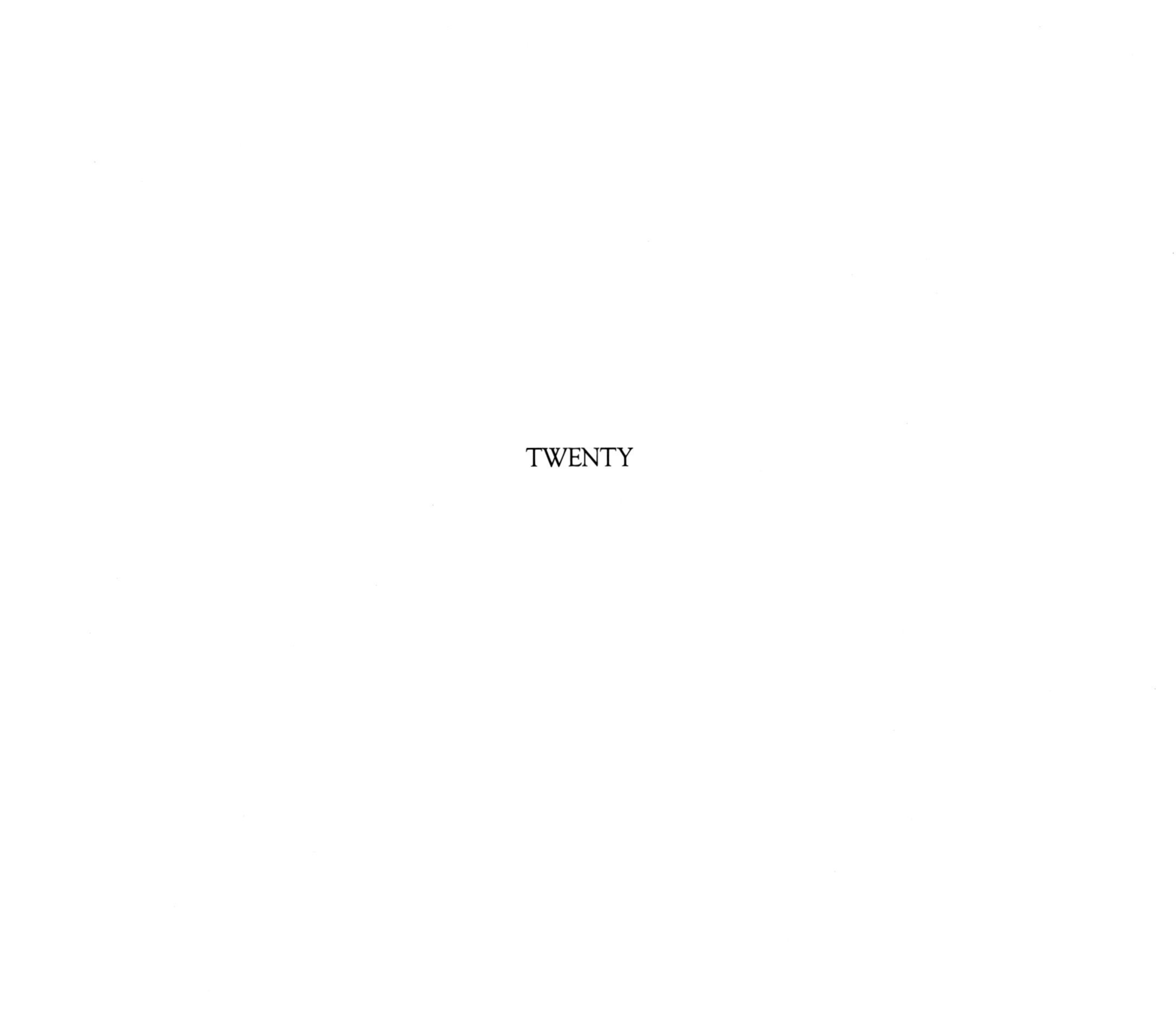

TWENTY

MAGIC ECHO

Lost violins float back to the cloud
Still playing echoes of the concerto,
Flying on wings of unheard music
That still haunts the last stone castle.
She has looked from the dream of parapets
Out across the landscape of culture,
And the stagecoach has left with her body.
Music is an insubstantial persistence
That crosses wastes of silent desert,
And memories are a melodic echo
Of insistence on past centuries.
Song is not a missile, no space machine,
But violin of ancient wood and varnish
Of man's blood that carry generations.
Soul is the lone, solitary listener
As instruments float back to heaven.

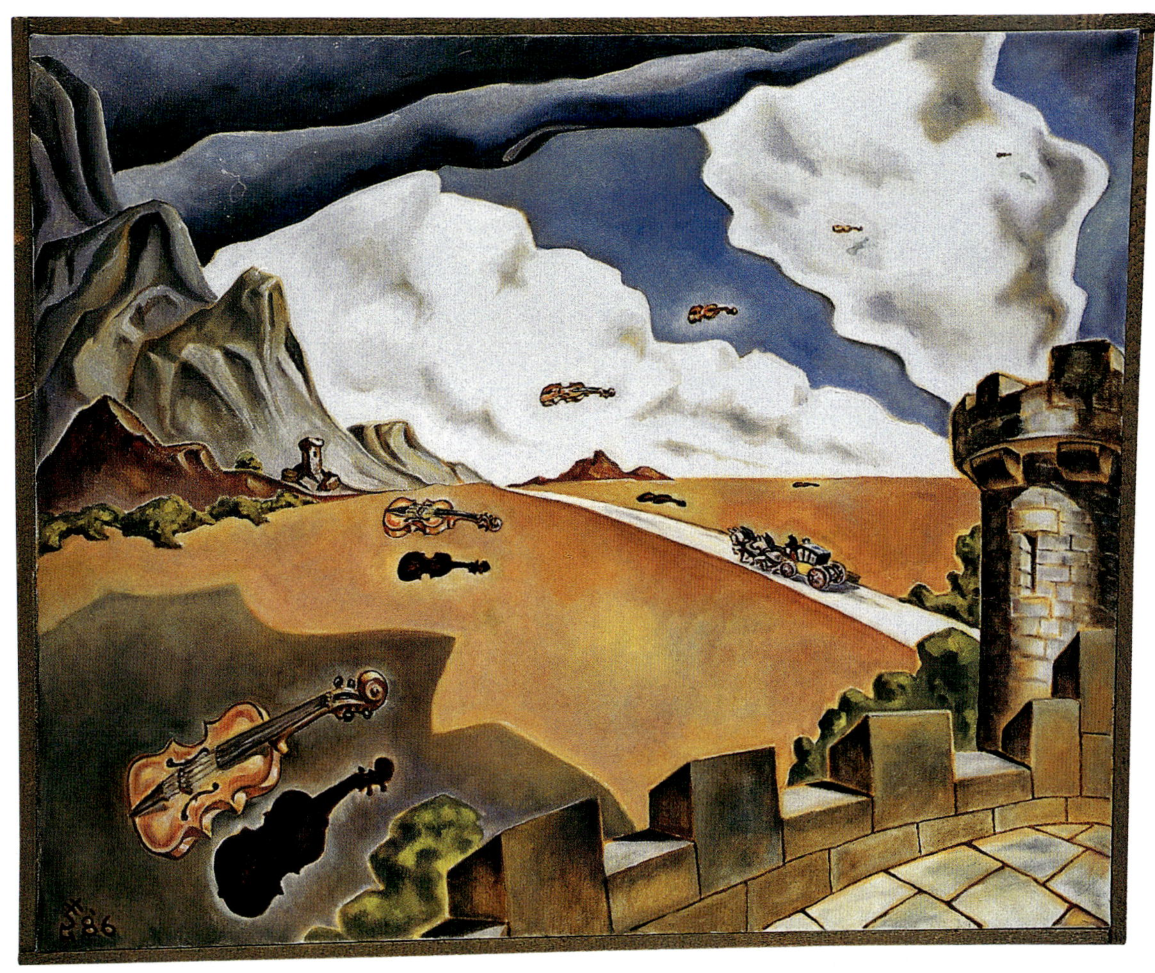

Magic Echo 30" x 24"

TWENTY-ONE

MOONSTRUCK

Mr. and Mrs. Moose at the opera
Show their homage to each other
Just like Mr. and Mrs. Smith at night
In their parchese hairdos and suits.
The foyer is witness to animal love
As the couples of middle class
Show animate devotions in the glass.
Mr. Moose is on his knees remembering
The proposal to the lady with antlers,
For all couples are on the same steps —
This is where we show our inner life,
The horns that no one ever sees,
The head of moose in the mirror.
Yes, Mr. Moose says, "Do you remember?"
And she nods with a thrill, "Oh, yes!"
For they are just their disguise at the opera
After coming for the barbecue and grille.

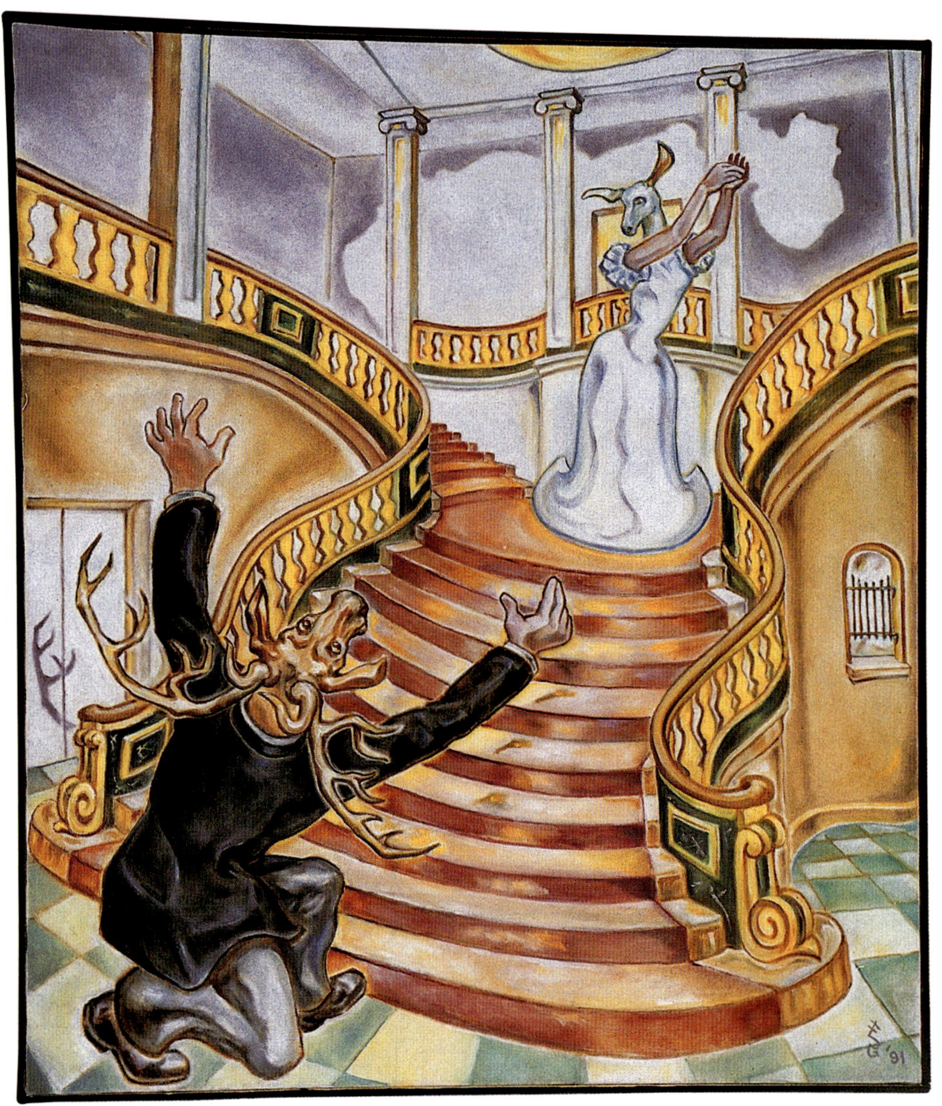

Moonstruck 30" x 34"

TWENTY-TWO

ACTION/ABSTRACTION

At dance school I rehearsed myself,
Scanning my own body in the mirror,
Punctilious to the eternal physique
As I stretched the legs of my being.
Enchanted by shadows of myself
I moved in abstractions of the body,
An image in my own eyes, Narcissus himself.
It was the wild sex of abstraction
That mesmerized me with dancing shoes,
For I was limber and had nothing to lose.
When I was young the walls reflected me,
I never asked the question, "Who are you?"
But I danced for everyone to see,
Reveled in my own refreshment.
Choreography of my own identity
Was all I lived to move and interpret;
The rest was a mere abstraction.

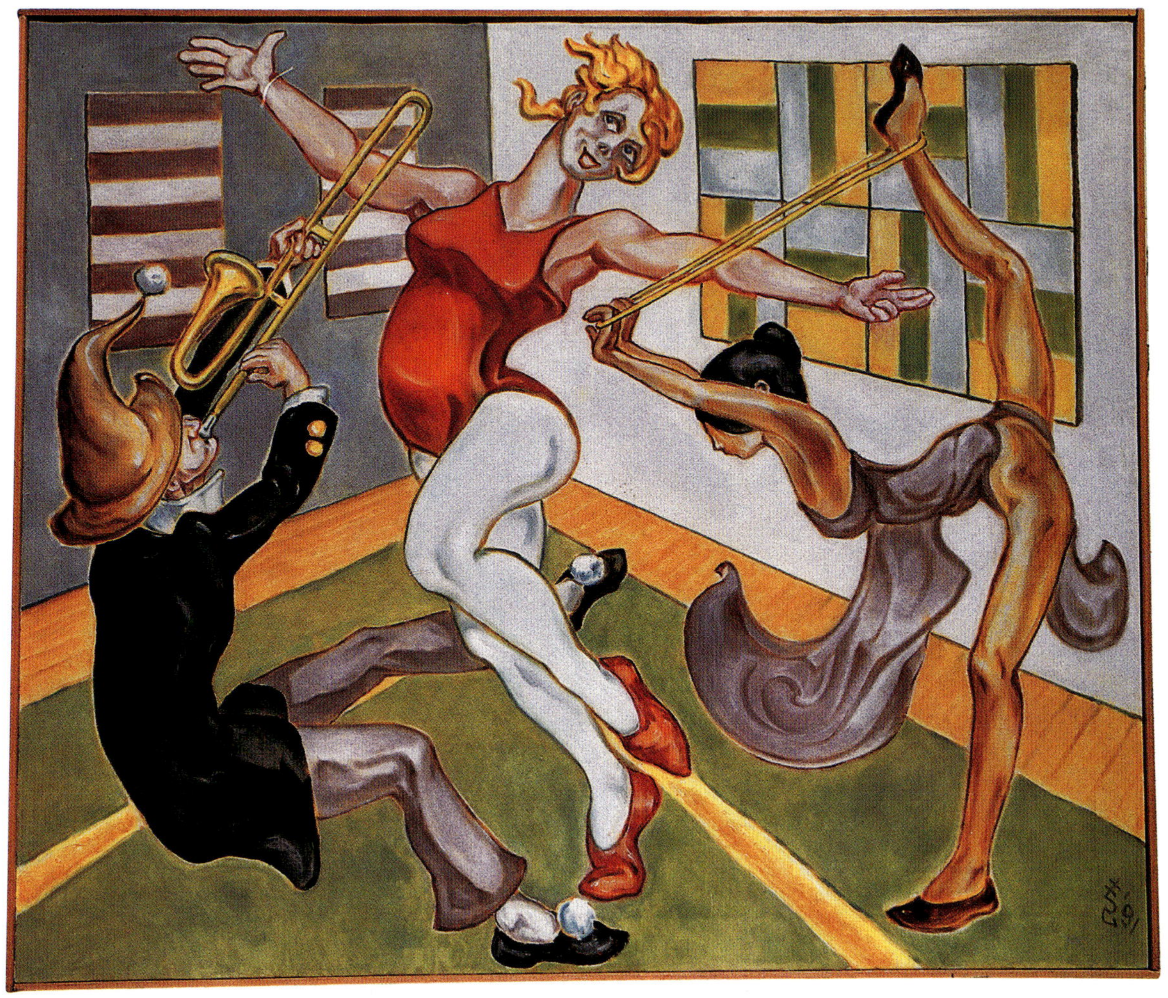

Action & Abstraction 34" x 28"

TWENTY-THREE

GRAND STAIRCASE STOMP

This was Mr. Curator of the Met
Coming from his office to the latrine.
This was where he could do the act
Alone, in the mirror, unseen.
His taste was a dance unto itself,
Venus with her head blown off in victory,
And on the black and white checked floor
He was looking out for more — more of himself.
He had become an art work in his own honor,
A model of his own ornate opinion,
And millions of viewers who came to the museum
Came to see the curator's own inner life.
The daintiness of him was a tapestry,
Yes he himself was his own statue in the hall.

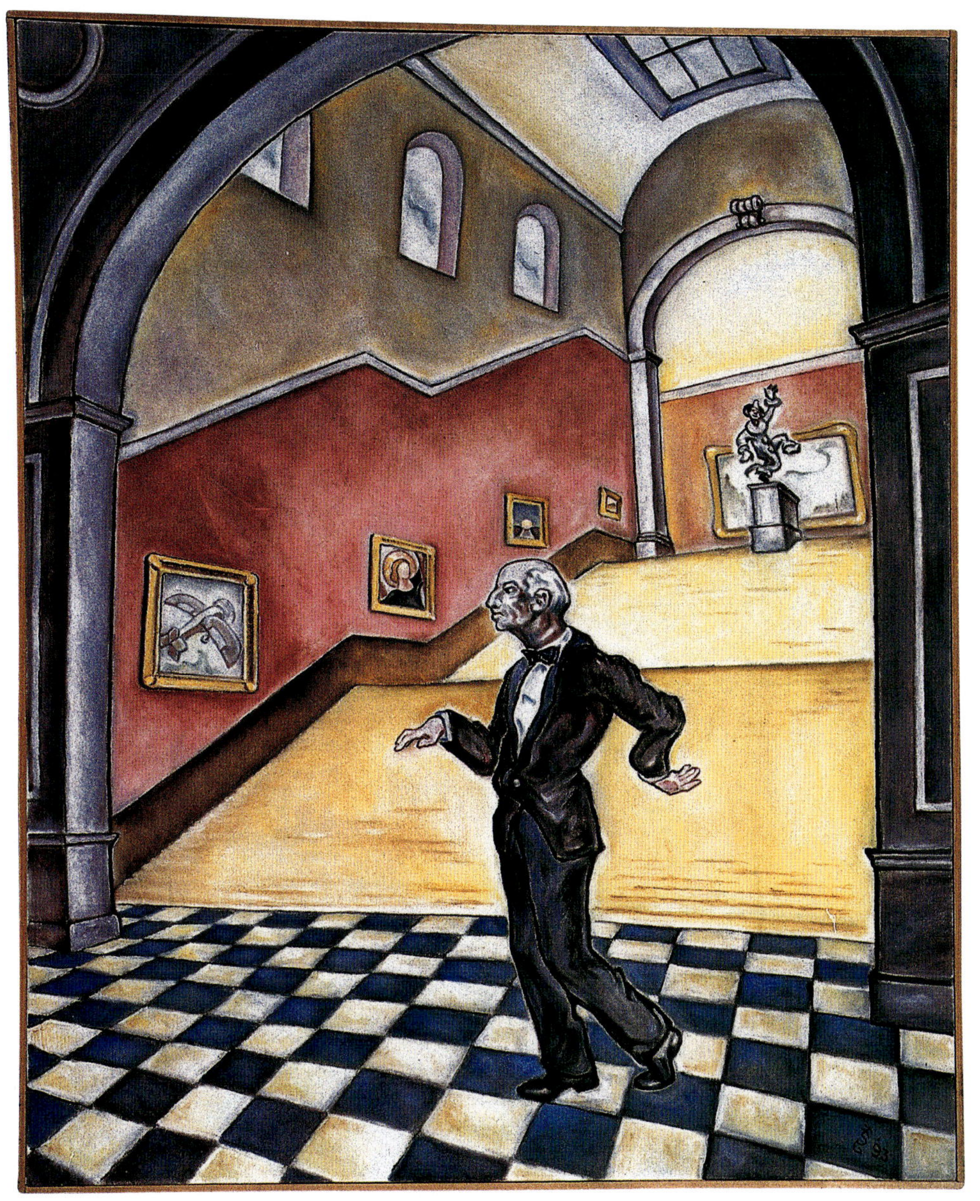

Grand Staircase Stomp 28" x 34"

TWENTY-FOUR

DANCING INTO MIDNIGHT

The waitress danced into midnight
Like some moonlight for sale,
A chorus girl from the restaurant
In bloomers that barely covered her tail.
She greeted the recalcitrant spirit of love
As if she could cast her charm on the street,
And the old man before the white church
Has asked her to marry his old age.
The purpose of work is to reach the nuptials
And be embraced by the golden ring,
And her blond hair is not half so real
As the ceremony of the marital thing.
She will sweep the very streets for him
And vacuum away all the clouds
And iron off the wrinkles of things,
And she will dance with herself if she must.
Yes, she takes the big tips or goes bust,
Oh there she goes the sweetie pie
With her long hard legs up into the sky.

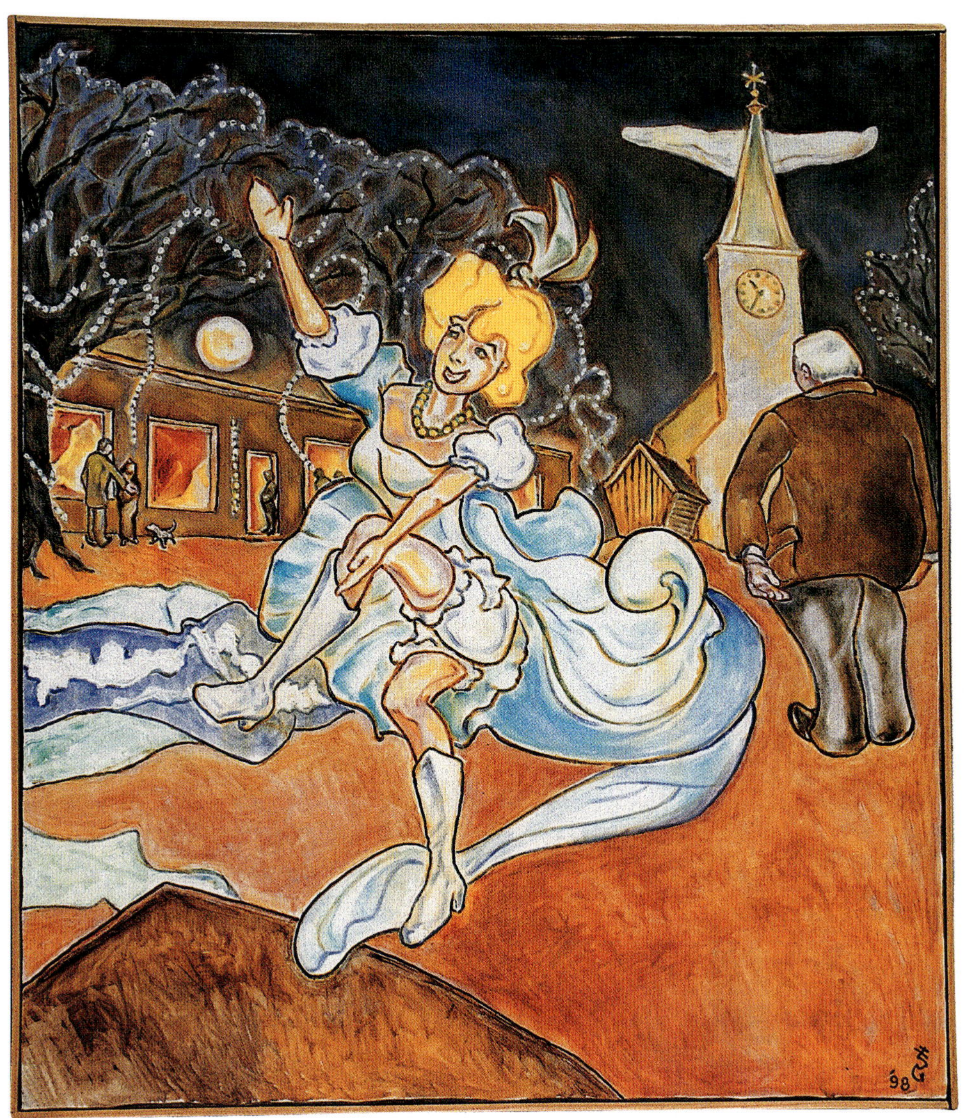

Dancing Into Midnight 28" x 32"

TWENTY-FIVE

ISLAND MAGIC

Would that I thought as the evening star
Something near and something afar,
Could be as the seas be, a shell,
Die, and yet still live to tell.
Could be as the evening darkness is,
Hers in the sand, surf being his,
Could look like the moon from out the sky
And hang in heaven just like an eye.
Could blow in the wind like the uplift palm,
Lie like the island sweet and calm.
Would that I were a sunlit lizard
Alive in the sand like a wizened wizard;
Love would come like a stolen wind
Changing its breath like a girlish mind.
Would that I thought as the evening star
Something near and something afar.

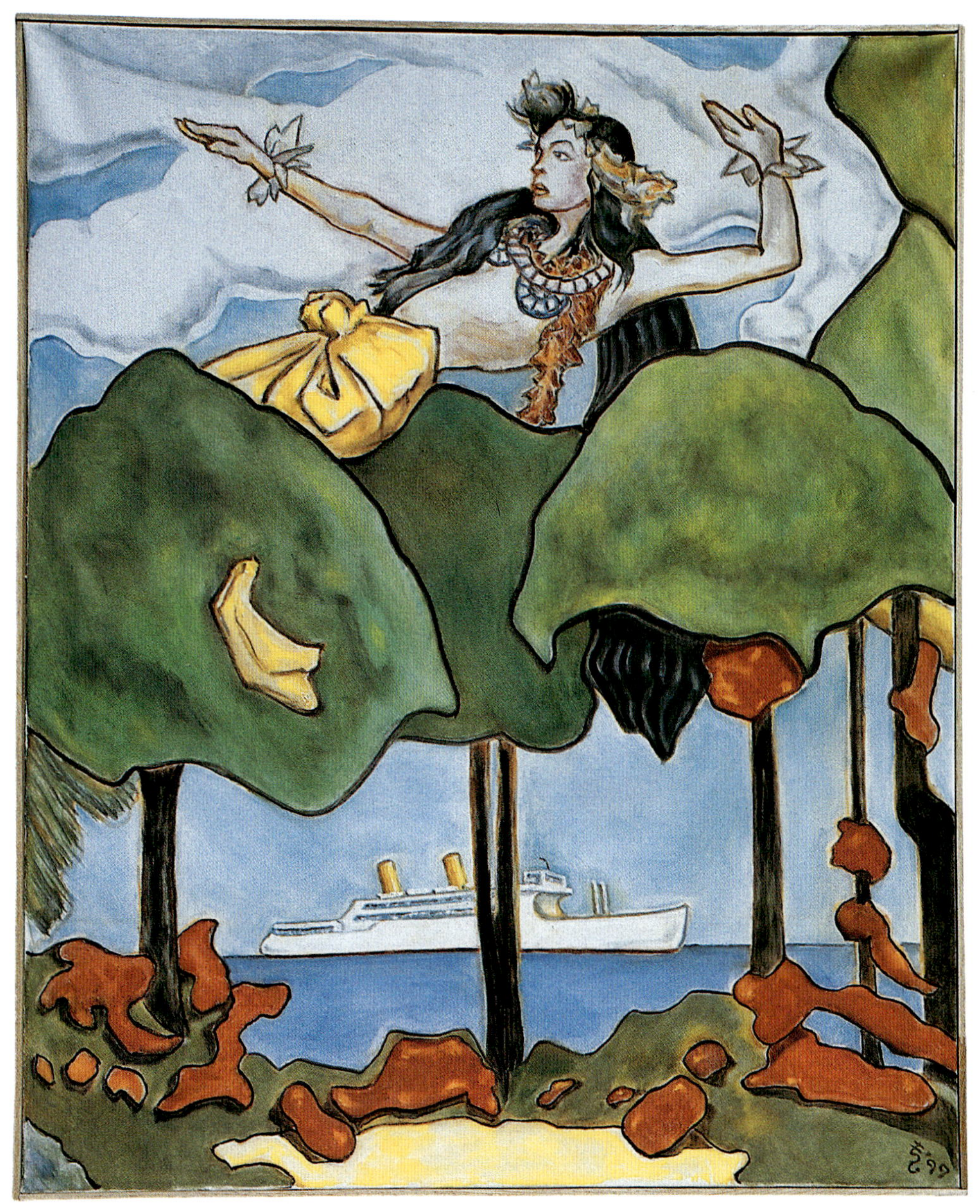

Island Magic 38" x 34"

TWENTY-SIX

RETREAT

Round, round world is his naked head
Through the window of searing light,
Iron bars the flagrant shadow,
Yes, at noon, it is exactly bright,
Oh, Vincent! Alone in the colored corner,
Bare crucifix for an only friend,
You spoke to the unpainted flowers,
And the whole landscape hallucinated.
I have sat on the very same chair
In the utmost of your isolated despair,
In the same cell of ultimate vision
Longing for a woman and the café
Writing letters to a brother far away.

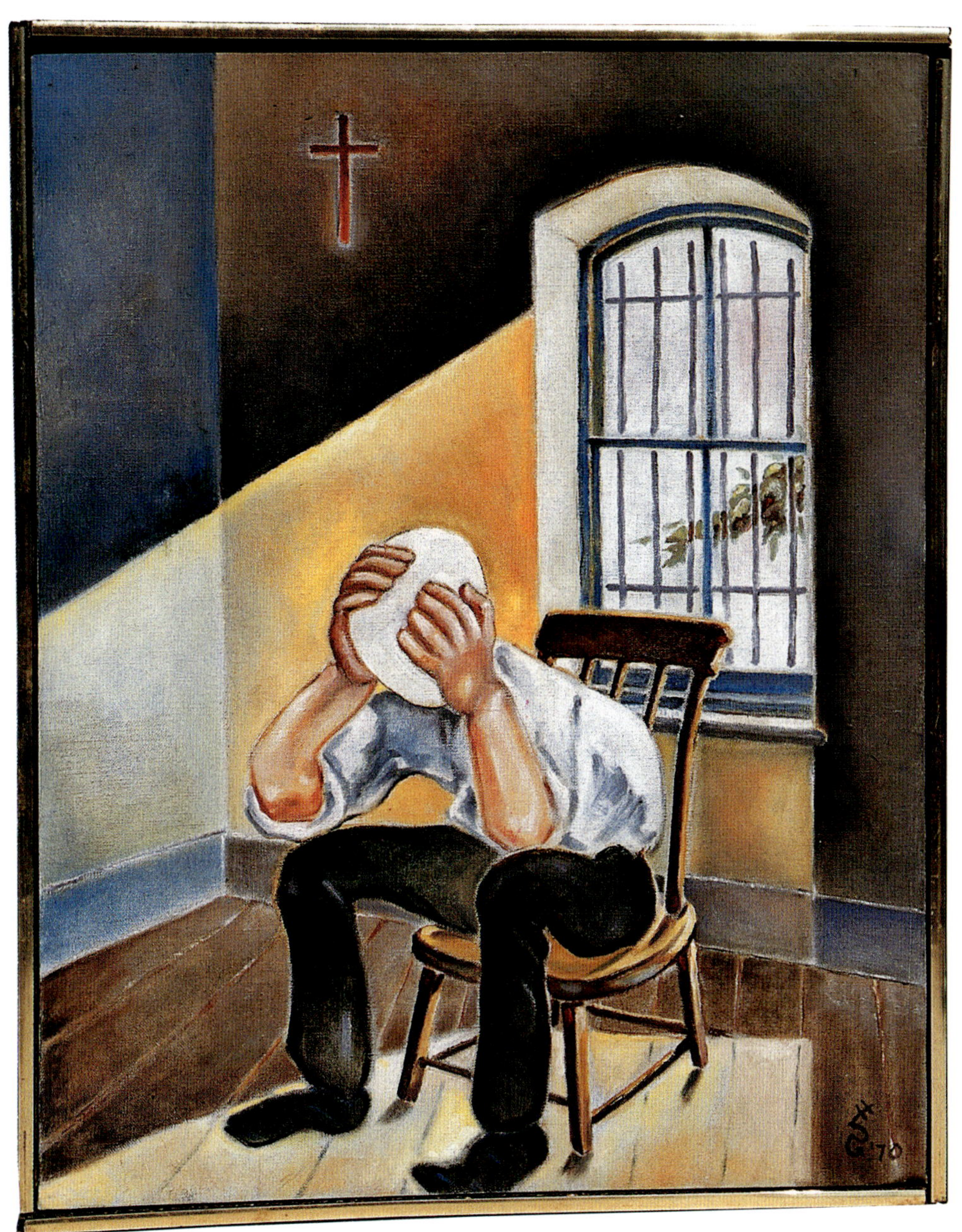

Retreat 16" x 20"

TWENTY-SEVEN

DRAGONS' TEETH

The beatnik of peace plows earth
Where tombstones mark dead ideas
And the black angel of premature death
Guides the plowshare in its furrow.
Each gravestone a petal of unlove
Left by the brooding culture of war,
Each poem of a shortened life
Dug under by the oxen of old.
The landscape becomes a monument
To the death of ideas, of notions,
Sacrificed by nations, of the once young.

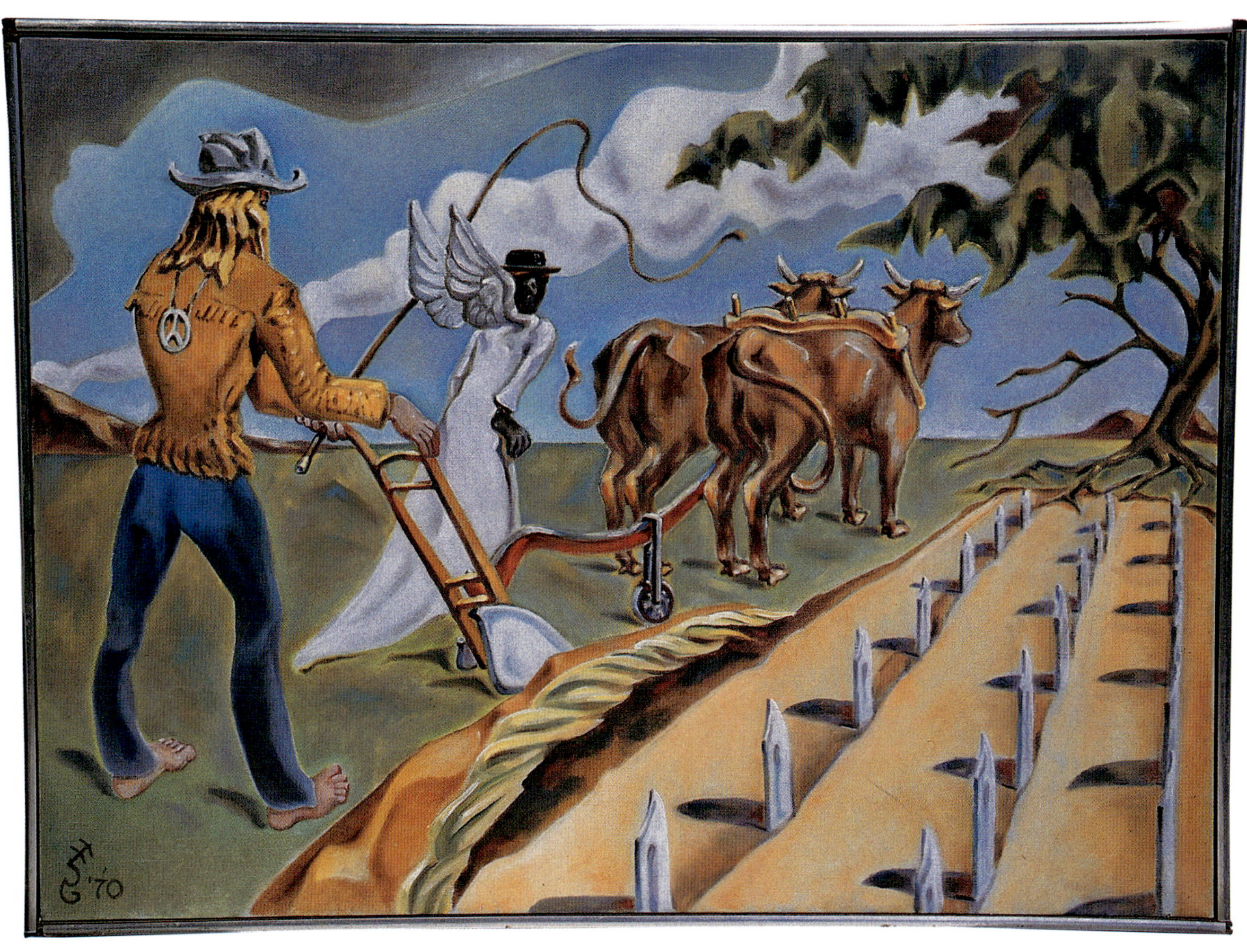

The Dragons' Teeth 28" x 20"

TWENTY-EIGHT

VEILED SYBIL

Ghosts of the first forgotten nations
Haunt the primordial sky
As the veiled sybil, imprudent Patience,
The white girl who would never say die,
Sits in her ancient rustic rocker
And foretells the coming civilization.
The old dry ranches of X and Y
Stretch to the future roads and TV,
And the plains give away to dot.com,
But her man still rides the back of the wind
While Patience is the black widowed Mom.

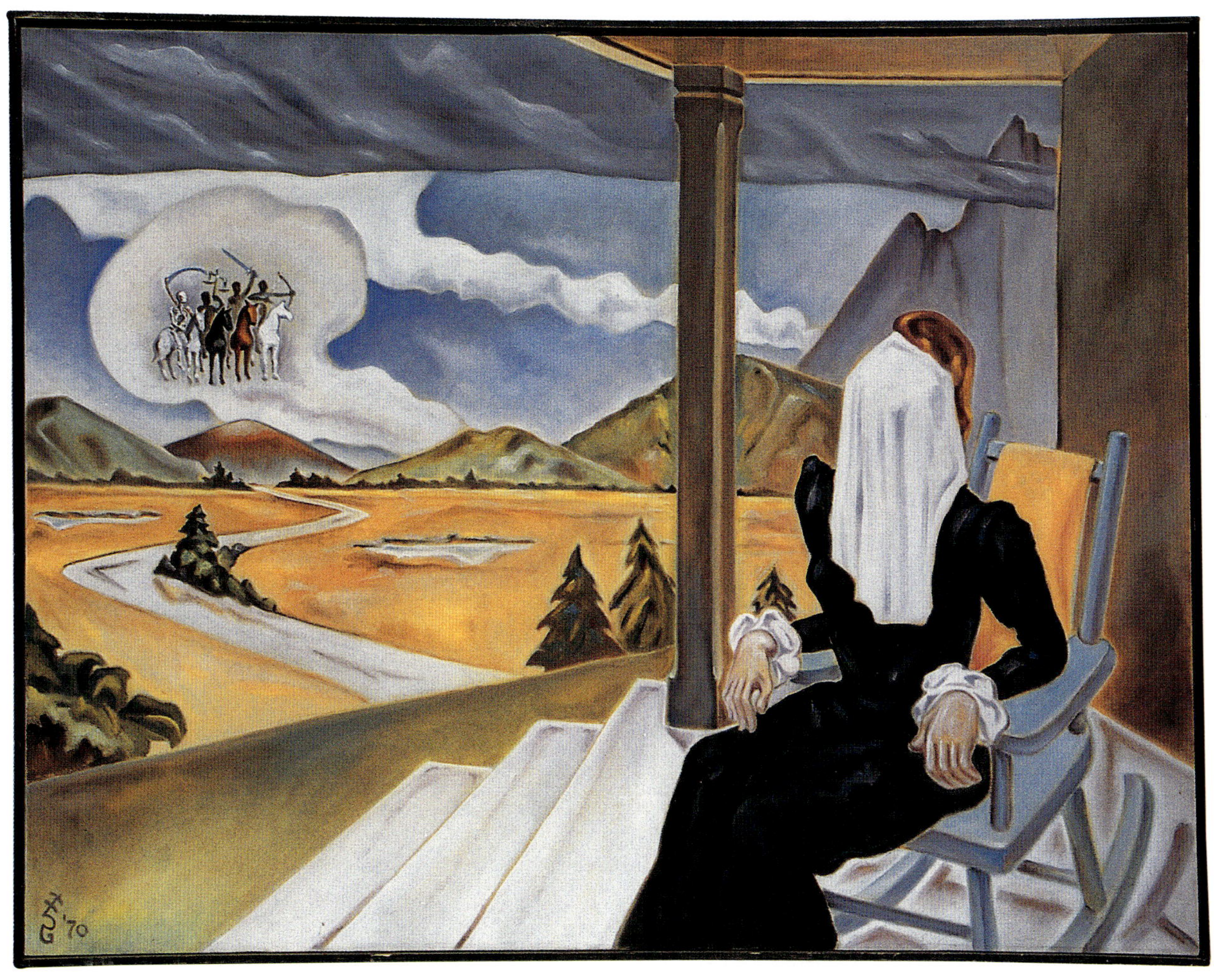

Veiled Sybil 24" x 26"

TWENTY-NINE

AUTUMN WALK

The old hag Halloween
Is walking down the path to winter
Turning the world of summer green
Into the bright foliage of Autumn.
Under her black pilgrim hat
Nests a bird of ominous ideas,
And through the rusty barbed wire
Crawls her invisible black cat.
Around her roll memories of New England,
Haunted prayers of religious freedom;
Mouse and bat worship as she goes
Brewing a future no child knows.

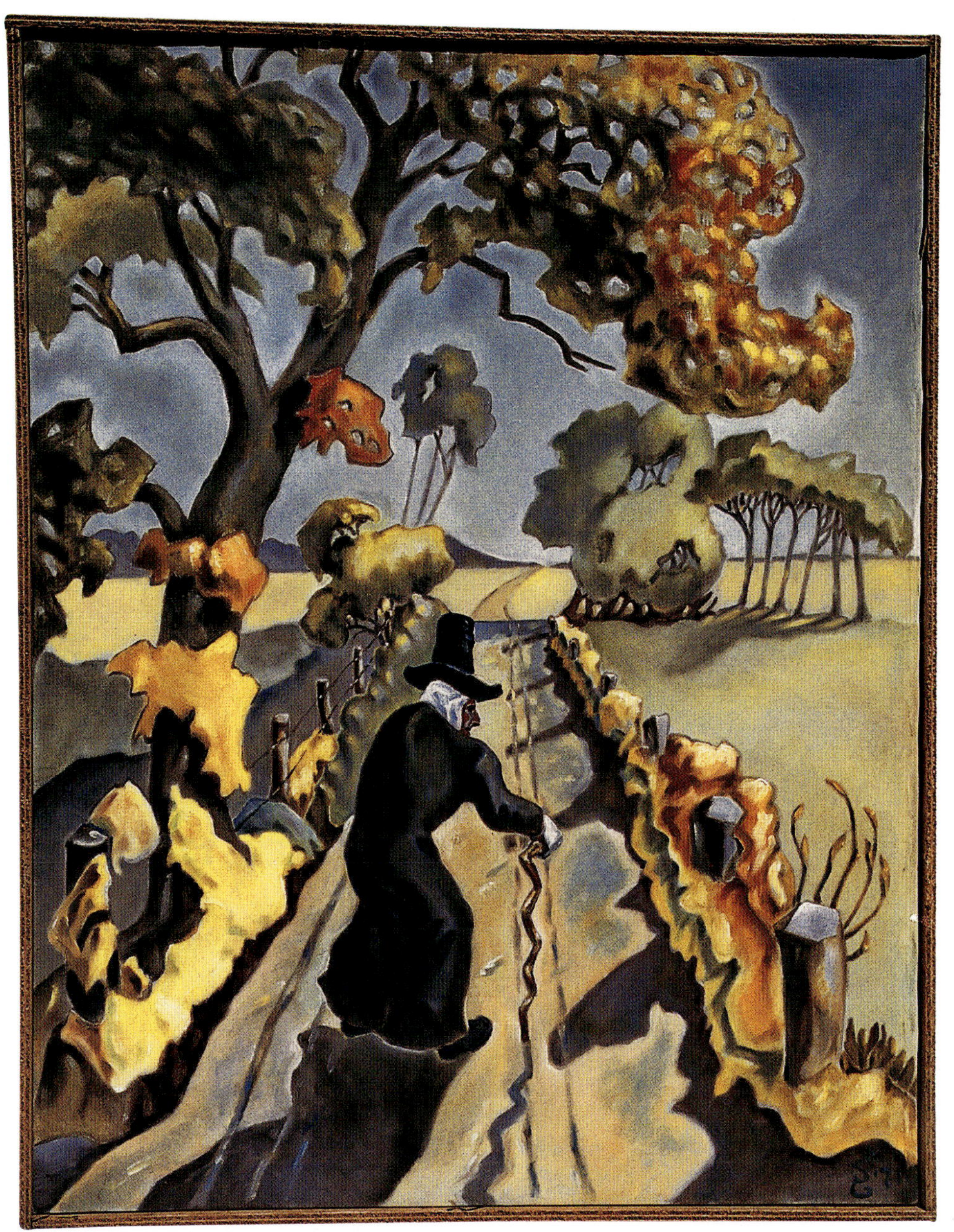

Autumn Walk 22" x 28"

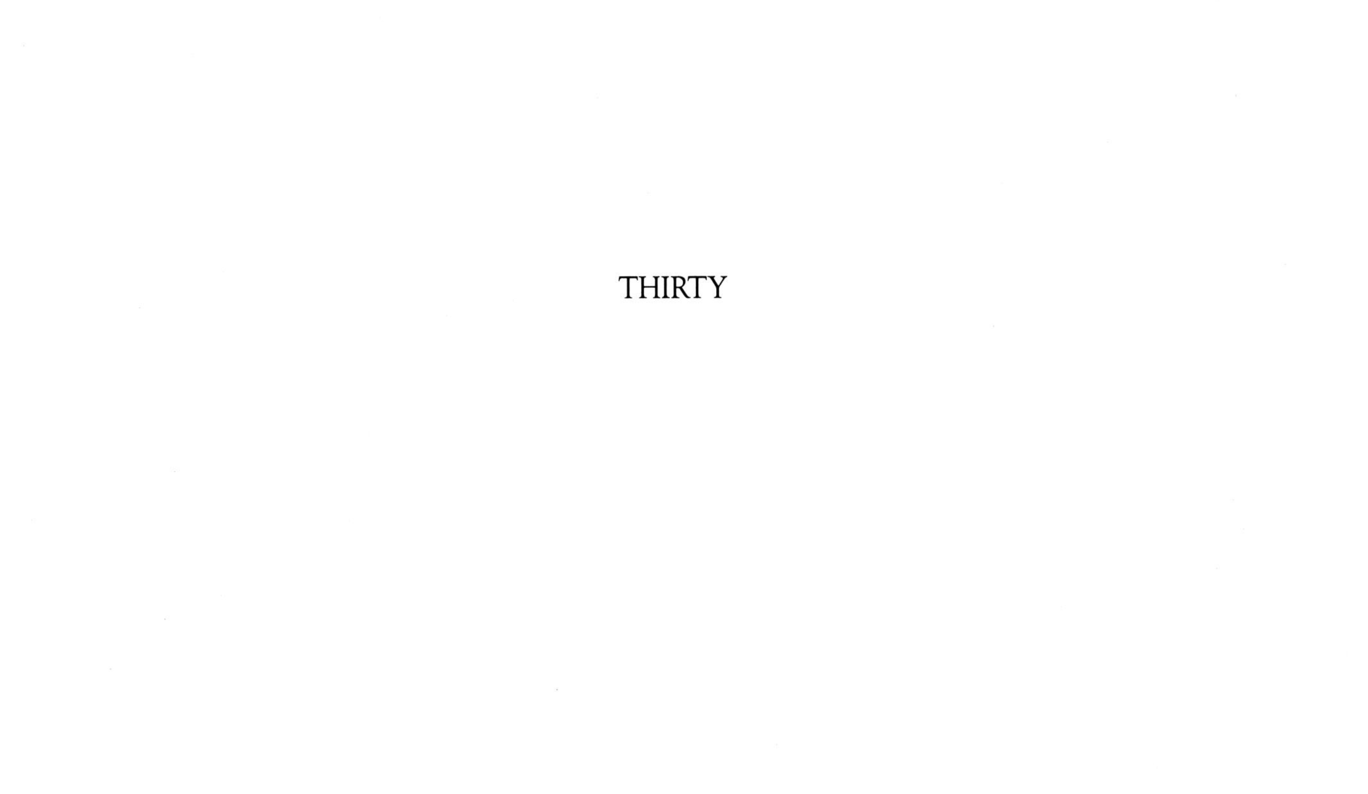

THIRTY

BRIMMING RIVER

Ancient time repeats on the Potomac,
Where among monuments of government
Salome's severed head predicts the future.
Don Quixote has met John the Baptist,
And Christ flows in the flooding waters.
Jesus is the name of the marble horse,
But yet to come to the future people
Are Washington, Lincoln, and Jefferson.
Her dark hair bodes darkly as she looks
Up into the secular heaven,
And under arched bridges murmur
Whispering waters: "America, Oh beautiful, save us!"

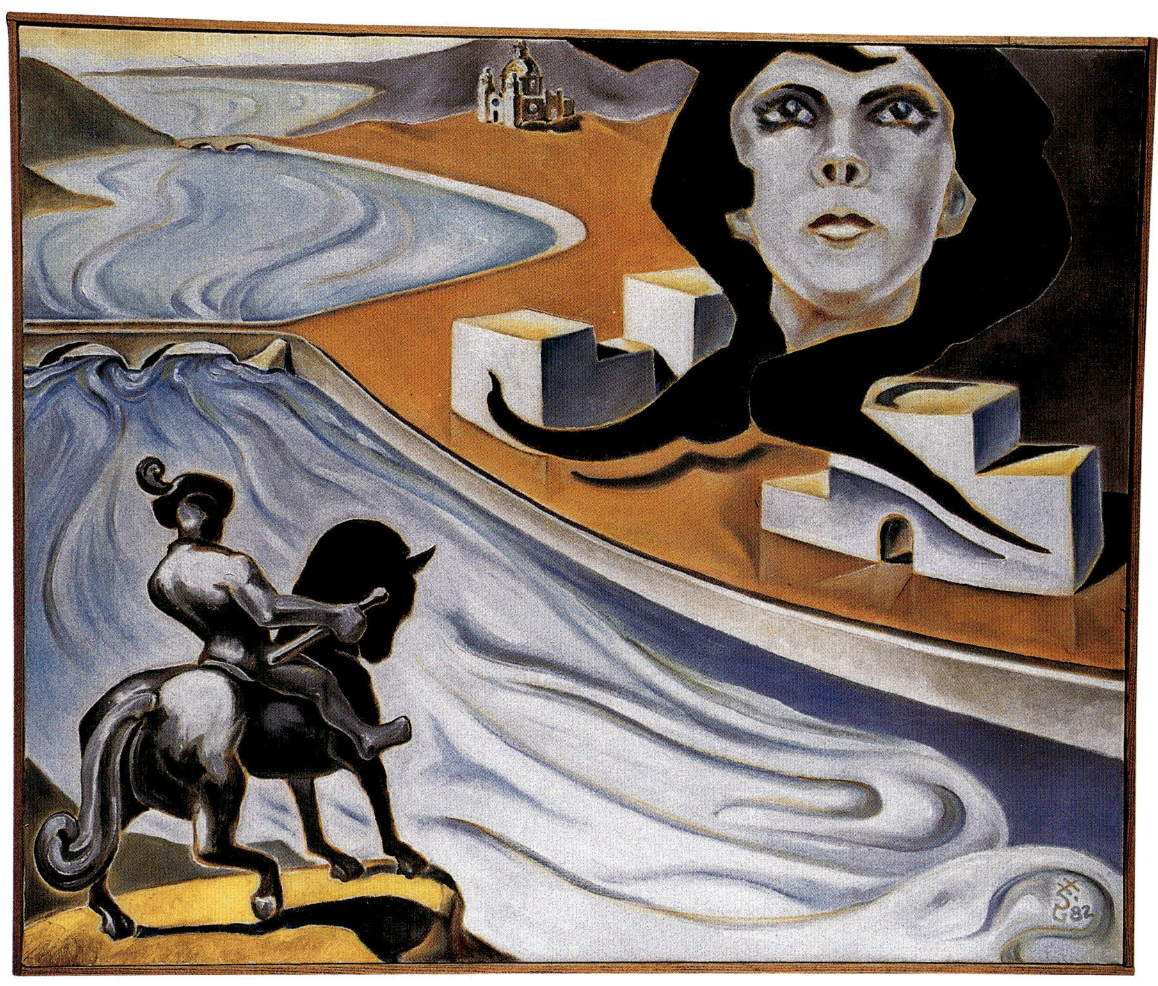

Brimming River 30" x 24"

THIRTY-ONE

WINDOW SHADE

The stars believe, a child of dreams,
From far above this earth's routine,
And on another galaxy
My love lives bright as spatial fire;
The stars believe and I do too,
In all she ever felt or did,
As if we two fell in the sea,
And love, a prayer, the fishes said;
As if we washed upon the beach,
Eternity stretched out on sand,
Two gulls of blue, blue paradise
Who fell from out of surf and salt;
The stars believe, the stars believe
In me and you upon the sea.

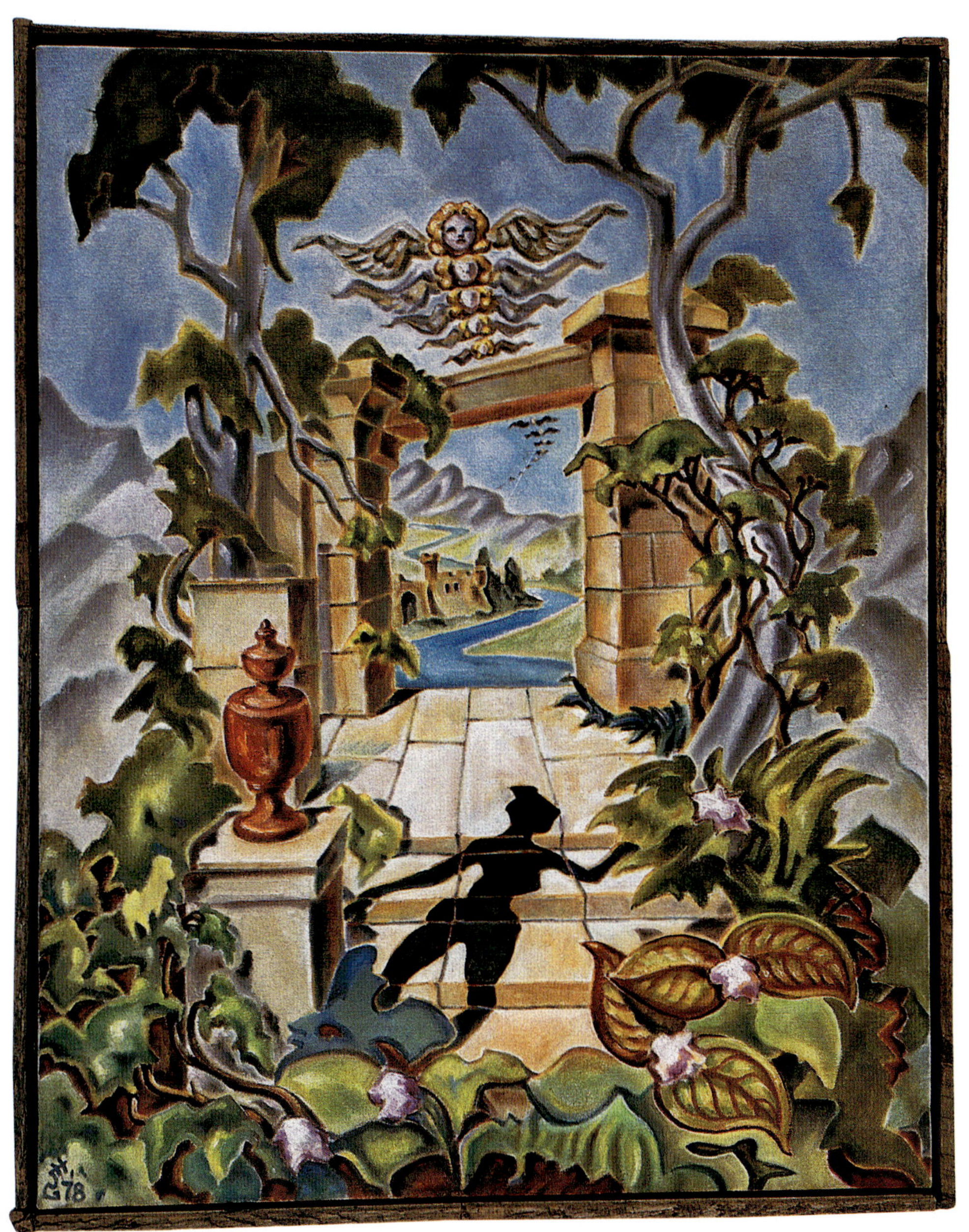

Window Shade 24" x 30"

THIRTY-TWO

MAGICIAN

Magician is the man mother married
Who leans now on an old root
And the tree of forest patriarchs
Grows behind him like a young shoot.
In old age he mumbles a spell
And whole cities suddenly crash;
With love, he says, not all is well,
But the gold, the gold is buried.
Will my grandchildren unseen
Find human treasure in earth
When the old magician himself goes poof,
And life vanishes from the darkling tree?

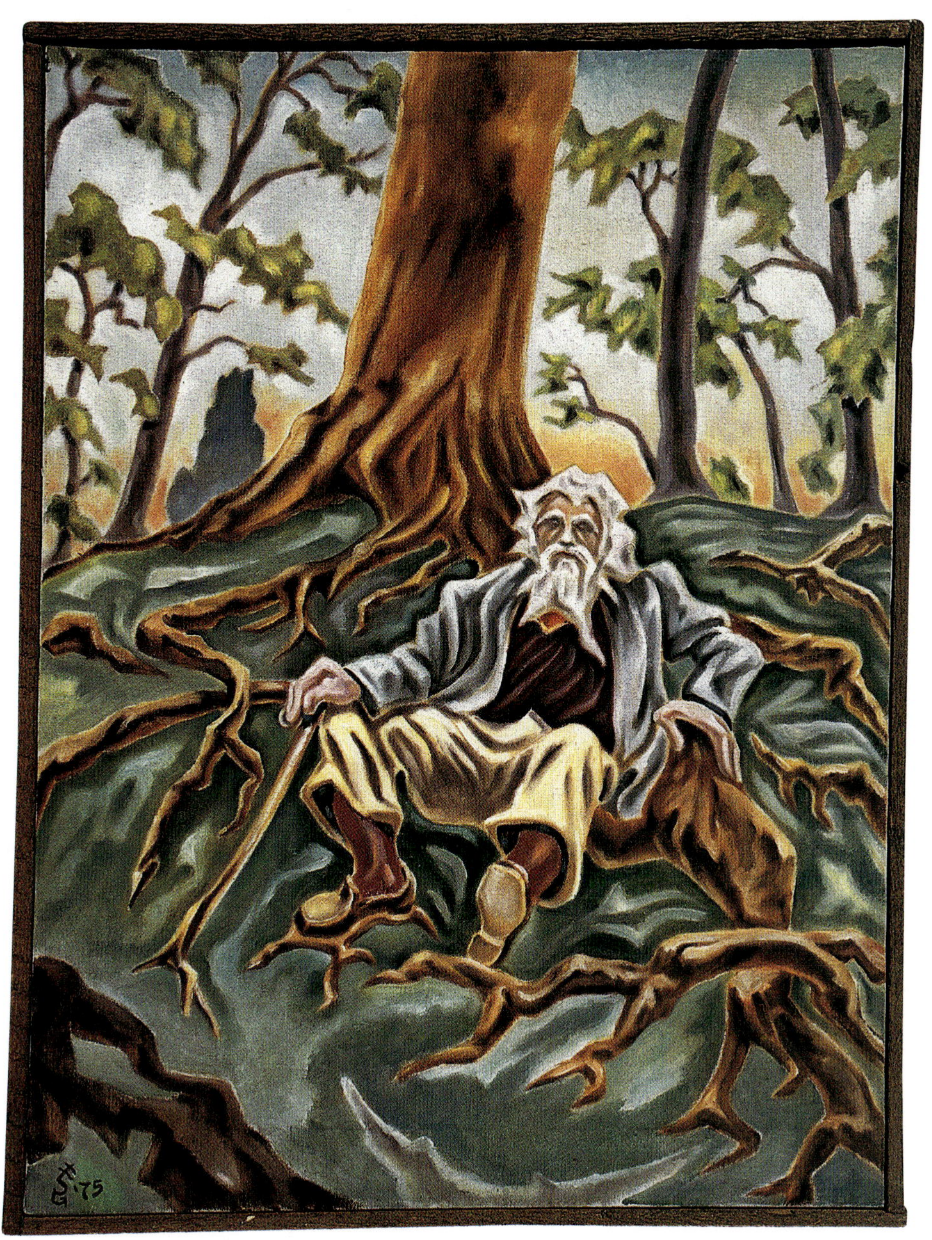

Magician   18" x 24"

THIRTY-THREE

THREE SHIPS AND A WHITE HORSE

The last white horse in the harbor
Comes to pay homage to Columbus,
And proud tall ships of a century past
Wave fond farewell to the white canvas.
The wagoneer has fought the Revolution,
And he hangs his head in a prayer
As ghosts of the wharves take the air.
There is nothing anymore the same there
Where history once disembarked,
Only the old custom houses
That once took their human toll,
And the poemful horse and its cargo.

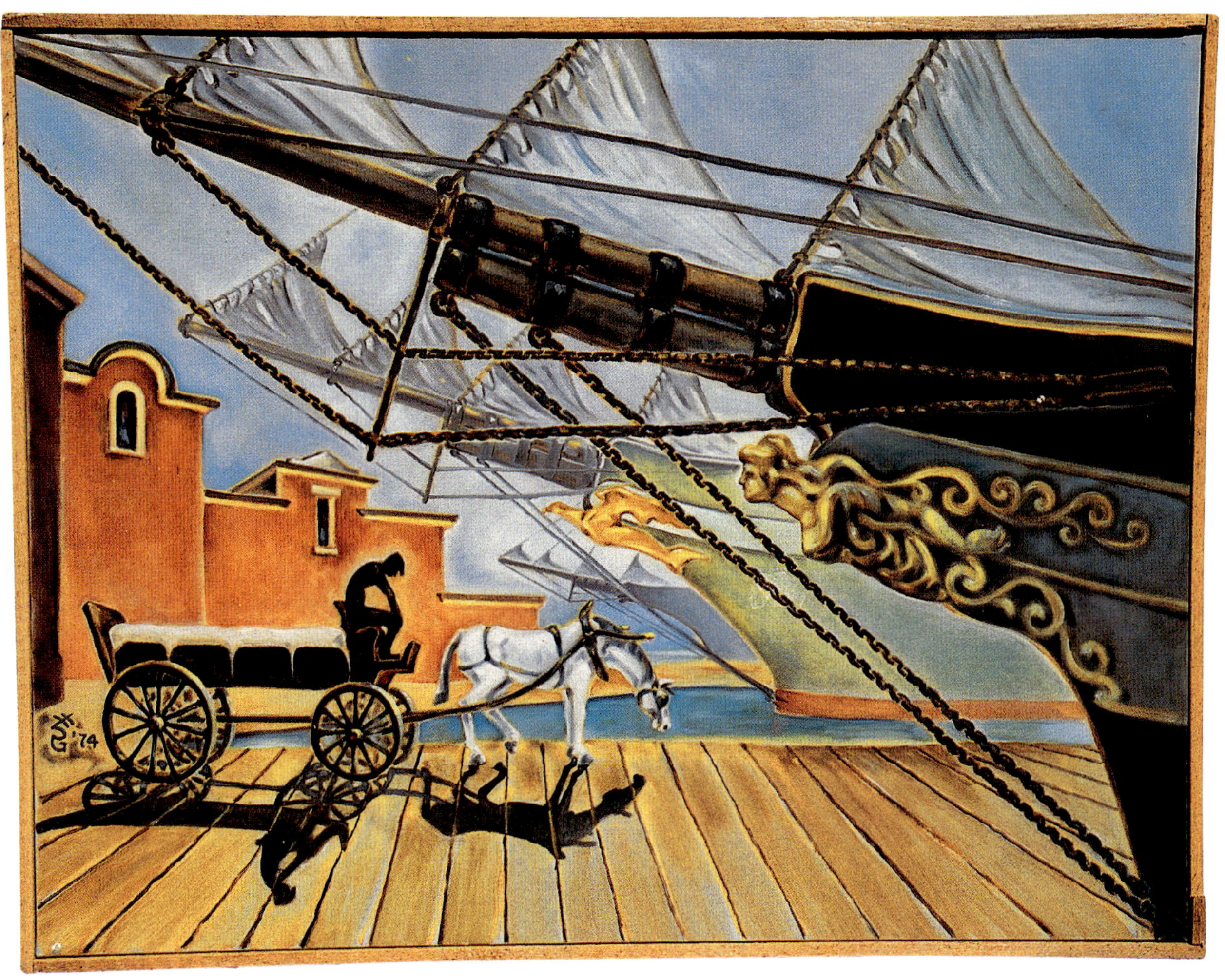

Three Ships and A White Horse 32" x 24"

AMERICAN ORIGINAL

A Memoir

by Rufus Goodwin

EXPERTLY he wields two canes like paint brushes but is still master of his own house, which, as an architect before turning to painting, he built sixty years ago on 15 acres; now, at an early American table where as a boy he saw President Theodore Roosevelt sitting with his own Dad, he has in a sense outlived his own house and the century — an authentic American pop magic realist.

Across the lawn, past a statue of a cigar store Indian, in the woods stands his own studio, with 500 pictures on canvas stored away that he has painted over the last thirty years. About 75 of them have been bought or given away. He was born in 1904.

His latest exhibition was mounted at the Canton Art Gallery in 1994, but he has shown in Paris, New York, at the Connecticut Goodspeed Opera House, in New Britain, and elsewhere. Connecticut Magazine did a cover article on him when he was ninety. Now, as he moves on, he still paints seven or eight pictures a year.

Jane Doe, of course, would be startled by his pictures and ask, "Why doesn't he paint flowers?"

Jane Doe might even find his images mystifying, a bit cantankerous, or even threatening. His strong point is not niceness. Not even color, although his acrylic palette boasts a certain low-keyed circus quality, but it is his architectonic composition, his draftsmanship, that is his strong point. Some of the pictures are almost large cartoons.

A lot of them are somewhat "literary" paintings, in the sense that they say something about the American scene — references to the scene of 19th and 20th century Americana.

But it is a surrealist pop scene. Literary pop art. The paintings comment, record, remark, mock, satirize, and celebrate.

Yet they are also sometimes lyrical. Violins float in heaven. Television sets wash up on the beach. Horse and carriage go down the road next to automobiles. Daniel Boone and J.P. Morgan reappear mythically. Superman and Mickey Mouse and Che Guevera make appearances, but so do sailboats, Victorian salons, women in buss dresses, Greek temples, New England mansions, ghosts, and much more.

It is a sort of lyric literary pop surrealism that he likes to call magic realism, a North American version. Although he insists that he paints as he sees, this visual world of his is both journalistic and fantastic at the same time. "But Dad," I say, "What about Jane Doe?"

"Well," he says, "she's not educated to look at it. Victor Gombrich, the art critic, tells the story of an Italian group of students in Michelangelo's time who were looking at Egyptian sculpture. They were all laughing at all the views of profiles and saying the Egyptians don't know how to paint. The Egyptians are uneducated. But it was the students themselves who didn't know what to look for in the Egyptian friezes. They were the ones who were uneducated."

He picks up a greeting card from the Red Farm Studio Collection, a commercial collection, that is benefiting the Mystic Seaport.

The picture on the front is BLUE STAIRWAY AND BEGONIAS, quite pretty, by John Atwater, 42' x 54', in oil. The caption describes the picture as one of the weathered deck and stairway behind the Captain's quarters in Stonington where the proprietor tends a glorious collection of flowering begonias, geraniums, and fuschia.

The card says: "The beauty of this tranquil scene is quite inspiring — the lush colors, the repetitive patterns of the woodwork, and the striking play of the sunlight with the shadows."

"Atwater is an able artist," Dad says, "but it's boring. There's not much imagination."

"But Jane Doe likes it," I say.

"It's too comfortable. She doesn't have to learn anything. It looks exactly like she'd like it to look. It doesn't make her a bigger person."

"So that's why you don't paint pretty pictures? So Jane Doe will become a bigger person?"

He looks a little miffed. "I think some of mine are pretty."

Then he hands me a few postcards of Currier & Ives from the 19th century.

"The Currier and Ives realism captures a part of the life at the time, something of the United States. It looked a little like that."

"Well," I say, "why don't you do that? Why don't you make pictures that look just like the scene? You're always commenting. You juxtapose things real and unreal and then make a visual comment on the scene."

"I create the scene," Dad says.

And so he does. It may not look like Currier & Ives, but it does look like some of 20th century America with a keen eye for traces of the Victorian past.

Pictures, he says, "won't mean anything anyway to people until they know what they're about - like a Picasso or a Mondrian. That - to say what the pictures are about - he says, is what art history and criticism are for.

Gombrich, he says, said that you have to have the idea of what you're looking at; then he tells the story of the young boy whose mother was trying to get him to eat his vegetables.

It was broccoli. "What is it?" The young boy asks. "It's broccoli," says the mother. "Well," says the young boy, "I say its spinach, and I say, 'To hell with it.'"

It reminds him of another story.

"I was climbing the steps to the gallery," he says, "with my two canes, and this man came up to help. 'I'm a handicapped artist,' I told him. 'I can see that,' the man says, 'you have two canes.' 'No. I don't mean that,' Dad tells him, 'I mean I'm old. I'm Protestant. I'm a Wasp. I'm white. I'm pretty comfortably off. I'm not a woman. I'm not Black. I'm not Hispanic. I don't have AIDS and I'm not gay. That makes me handicapped in the art world.'"

He thinks about this for a moment. "I've stopped telling that story," he says. "They say I should be careful whom I tell it to."

"Maybe," I say. "But it's sort of true."

"Still. It's not nice," he says. There is a side of him, art notwithstanding, that still wants to be nice. It ran in his old Hartford family. I look at him in the dining room he built sixty years ago with the antique blue glass sherry decanter on the sideboard, and a picture of his own father as a young boy, later a Republican State Senator, looking down.

Sometimes, after talking, he likes to say, "Well, now that we've solved all the problems of the world, I guess we can go to bed."

Yes, an American original. Now, his own pictures stretched across the century, he seems to be making a mental and visual note of a hundred years. Though the museums may not have recognized it, I want to assure him he's an authentic, maybe even a great — not just a Sunday — painter. He has a vision. We both now it's true, in a way, but in the end it's probably Jane Doe who has the final word, some critic, or some promoter. I'm thinking now not just of the pictures, though, but the way he likes to be a cipher and use expressions sitting there like: "Oh, that's old hat," he'll say of some art, or that, when it comes to a new picture he likes, he'll say, "I'm just as pleased as the Dickens."

He paints at least a lot more pointedly than Churchill did. And his pictures are fun. They startle you. A violin playing alone in a graveyard. Or two moose greeting each other on the grand staircase of the Goodspeed Opera House. Or Superman toying with Mickey Mouse.

Or sometimes it's just a catboat from the 19th century waters sailing blithely through the dangerous ocean of the 20th century towards the Millennium. But today he is in good fettle, slacks, a sport coat, old leather vest, leathery shoes — he always has fine, new leathery shoes, usually moccasins. He is as lame as ever, of course, hobbling around, keeping a precarious balance, over ninety, carrying his "third leg," the wooden cane, which always drops when he is up to something, because he lets it go, or leans it on the furniture and it clatters to the floor. But I never pick it up because Dad doesn't like another body tending to his business.

He is not grumpy today and we immediately discuss Betty Friedan's book, THE FOUNTAIN OF AGE, which he says is quite sensible though she gets boring sometimes about how who spoke to whom and what they said.

But mainly she advises people to not think they're sick, to gamble on life, to risk being alive despite old age and, despite all, to stay out of the nursing home where they treat you as an invalid, or indulge your self-sorriness, or medicate you, and where you begin to lose belief in your powers and wither away and die. Dad isn't for that.

As for sex, Betty Friedan calls it intimacy, and this seems nice to Dad because nowadays sexuality means something that you do in-your-face before cameras or in the newspaper, and Dad says Friedan discourages the "bedtime athletes," urging instead companionship and reminding readers that what women like is someone with whom to share "emotions". Well, I tell Dad about things and read him some of my recent journal notes. I read him the notes, for instance, on the Boston University poetry reading under the direction of Derek Walcott and former poet laureate Mark Strand, and a profile of the poetess and slam artist Patricia Smith. He becomes concerned because suddenly I am talking about energy, burn, and heat, and he darkens considerably, warning me that Picasso, when he used African motifs for inspiration, never became black but remained Spanish-French.

I reassure him that although I am impressed by Patricia Smith, I would never imitate her — never could — and that my response to Derek Walcott would be, "Well, like it or not, white Charlie still has something to say."

"That's right," Dad says.

It is suppertime and the Avon Old Farms bar is closed for repairs so we go to Amarin's, a Thai place on the strip of route 44, and order duckling in green curry, with brown rice, and the waitress explains that Amarin is the legendary god who created "green and happiness". Well, I think, if only I could remember what we talk about at these suppers because, in the twilight of life, we pull out all the stops and chronicle the century.

He says some mischievous things, too. Like at the exhibition he went to last night, at the Town and Gate, a women's club in Hartford, when the hostess asked him what it was like, remembering old Hartford, being a member of old Hartford, to see the city today. "What is the new Hartford like, how are we doing?" She asked.

The question annoyed Dad because he thought they wanted to hear the usual pap about who was who and who wasn't, so he answered, "Well, I think we're doing pretty well. After all, we've had a black mayor for the last six years." And, of course, he says they were all sour at his answer. He lights up in a big smile as he says this.

We always go to bed early on nights like these, but despite twelve hours of rest, he is a little grumpy in the morning because he is clattering around in the kitchen trying to fix breakfast with two hands, hold his can the third, and walking on one foot.

"So what are we going to do for an encore?" I say, just to cheer things up. "Shall I get the bacon out?"

But he furls his great eyebrows, looks very cross, and growls, "Too many cooks spoil the broth. Go into the dining room, sit down, and read the newspaper."

Of course, it is an order, so I sit down in the dining room with its faded elegance, surrounded by John Marin watercolors, the portrait of Grandad, and the unpolished silver, and read in the New York Times how the President has said that the Free Trade Agreement is a world issue. The New York Times doesn't even front page the article.

I tell Dad about it and say I had listened to Clinton in 1992 repeating so often, "Have the courage to change," that though I usually vote Democratic, I pulled the Republican lever that time.

"I usually vote Republican," he says, "but I thought change was important that time and voted for Clinton. So we both voted for the same thing."

"Yes," I say. "Change."

"But our votes cancelled each other out," he says.

"Yes," I add, "and Clinton certainly gave us some more of the same old thing with a few new twists."

I rile Dad a little by saying that I admire Clinton somewhat because of the virtue of his vices: for instance, a draft dodger, marijuana smoker, an adulterer, a real estate speculator, but that I consider him on the whole a good high school council president. "Can't we give Clinton an issue for Christmas?" I say plaintively.

Dad has nothing in mind so I suggest BST, the new bovine seratropin drug that makes cows produce up to forty percent more milk. "Genetically engineered food," I say. "How about that for an issue?"

Dad says it is not up to the government to say what the food should be and that it is a scientific question. "We've been breeding animals our way for hundreds of years to be what we want them to be," he says, "and in this case they give the cows dope and the cows produce more milk".

"It's not nature," I respond.

"It's a pretty murky boundary," he observes, "and not much different. Who knows where to draw the line?"

I point out that BST increases the incidence of udder infection and that because the cows get more udder infections, they also get more antibiotics. This makes the chemical industries happy but not the cows, and the antibiotics get into the milk, and then either people drink the antibiotics or they throw the extra milk out. Either way the small farmer gets hurt.

But Dad doesn't think the issue will wash. He asks me how Yeltsin is doing.

"Pretty well. He's decided not to run again. Pretty smart. He says what he has seen in one lifetime is already too much for one man."

That brings up infotainment, which I tell Dad is the new business of newspapers because they have run out of hard news. And they no longer know what a news story is because nothing like World War II happens anymore. Dad looks sour and scours the Hartford Courant and says, "Is that why the lead story in the Courant is about a woman who was misdiagnosed as having AIDS and lived in fear of death for three-and-a-half years, taking twenty-seven drugs?"

"Exactly," I say. "It should have been the global issue NAFTA, but they put the misdiagnosed woman up front because she's more entertaining."

"Well," Dad says, "how about this item on page two about Patti Davis, Reagan's daughter, getting a marriage license from the justice of the peace? It's in 'People in the News.'"

"That's okay," I say, "but right under it is that Swiss girl, Heidi Fleiss, who ran the girlie racket in Los Angeles, telling Chung on the Today show that more than one thousand men were involved, and they're the ones who should be scared, not her. I mean, she's an attractive Swiss girl. She's the real news. She belongs on page one."

By this time we have eaten our eggs. Dad cooks them ranch style, sunny side over in the bacon grease; he learned it out West, and they are tasty, but the bacon is never cooked crisp because Dad is scared of dirtying the frying pan, which is the same reason he never cooks scrambled eggs. He doesn't like washing up the mess. He holds his figure by never eating butter, either, just two pieces of dried toast with English marmalade on it. Usually he listens to a little radio during the meal, wonders why the news announcers have such corny voices, and then lets the public radio play some music. He used to play violin himself.

But this morning I point out that the Russians have announced that they would use nuclear weapons first in case of an attack and that our President now plans to schedule new nuclear tests because the Chinese have exploded another bomb. Besides, the Russians used thousands of soldiers, exposing them to radiation, as guinea pigs.

"I ask you honestly, Dad," I say. "Do you think these men who lead us

and develop these weapons are mentally sick? You know, I mean insane?"
Dad looks hurt. He thinks about it awhile. Then he says, "Insane, no.
But sometimes they have bad judgement."
"Twenty five times enough bombs to annihilate each other? I think they
should be put away." Dad looks hurt. He picks up a piece of toast gently.
"Here", he says, "don't you want another piece of toast?"
The subject changes to rape. I tell him I have been put in my place on
Columbus Day weekend because I was at Charity's, and Sabrina, Doris,
and Constance were there, and I said, "I don't understand rape, do you?
I mean it's supposed to be a violent crime, but if it's really violent, how
can it be sexy? Besides, I've never understood how the rapist penetrates.
Under the best of conditions its hard enough to do with mutual consent."
But Charity and Constance put me down immediately and said it is the
easiest thing in the world to spread a woman's legs against her will. Charity
and Constance said I was totally out of order and changed the subject.
Dad gets a chuckle out of this and looks pleased. "Man proposes, God
disposes," he says, asking me if I have ever noticed that a woman can
target a man across a room and without saying anything, maybe wordlessly,
with some hidden body language or a shimmy of the eyes, get him to cross
the room and speak to her?
"I call it telkineticism," I say, "but let me ask you a question. Don't you
believe a woman in a living room with several young men present can get
one of the young men to utter her own thoughts, to speak up and say
what she is thinking? Women are sort of ventriloquists, don't you think?"
"No," says Dad. Then I point out that this is the very same way women

"That's all right," he says. "I remember that parable. I never understood why the Lord was so unforgiving. I mean, if you go to a tuxedo party, and you have no evening dress, you explain the situation. But the Lord was so unforgiving in the parable."

"That struck me too," I answer. "But the priest said that if the man had said he was sorry, he could have stayed."

"Of course," Dad says. "Priests always like it if you say you're sorry."

"The stranger in Camus' story was so incensed by the priest who came to his death cell demanding that

he apologize for killing an Arab that he wouldn't say anything at all to him, not even that he was innocent, to save his own life, so they guillotined him."

"Well," says Dad, "Camus' man was insane. He had a fit of anger against the priest."

"What struck the judge," I say, "was that the man smoked a cigarette during the wake for his mother. The judicial system in France, outraged by a man smoking a cigarette, is incredibly self-righteous."

Dad looks glum.

After a pause he says, "You know, I was thinking about the story you told last night about the poet laureate and the Nobel prize winner you listened to talking the Four Season's Hotel, and when there was a lull in the conversation, the Nobel laureate, gratuitously, said to the poet laureate, 'Fuck you,' just to see what the poet laureate would do. Well, he was trying to liven up the party. Some people, you know, talk that way. I mean, at breakfast they will say, 'Good morning. Fuck you.' It's part of their language. What did the poet laureate answer?"

"He said, 'What is this, part of a creative writing course you're teaching?'"

"Well," Dad says, "if you had said the same thing they would have thrown you out of the Four Seasons."

I smiled. "When you said at the exhibition that 'Hartford was doing pretty well, after all, they've had a black mayor for the last six years,' they would have called the attendant, too, if you hadn't said it with a smile. That's the thing about you, Dad, you use your charm and smile when you say those things, and they think you're not serious, but actually, you're just like me. You're actually serious."

"I was just mad they asked me about old Hartford," Dad says. "They expected me to mention your great-grandfather, J.P. Morgan's cousin, his first partner, actually, and tell them who is who.

"You know," I say, "someone has invited me to a slam poetry session down in New York. Fridays. Ten-thirty. An underground club. You get up on stage and someone gives you a topic, and you have one-and-a-half minutes to improvise a poem. It's like jumping off a cliff. The audience juries you. They asked me if I would do it. It's a stretch."

I can see Dad doesn't like the idea either. He asks me, "So what are you going to do?"

"I'm going to stand there for a minute-and-a-half and then say, I'm sorry. The muse isn't inspiring me just now."

"That's good," Dad says. "The trouble with slam poetry is it's like action painting. They're forcing it. No thought. I mean the Impressionists painted the spirit of the moment, too, but not off the top of their heads. They worked at it."

"You know what I'd do?" Dad asks.

"No."

"I'd take my clothes off."

I frowned. "That's what they want, Dad. They want goofy. They want an insult to classical poetry. It's their level."

Maybe neither of us have thought about it enough because slam poetry maybe really is about people being quick on their feet, rising to a level, getting their energy up, stretching, getting out of the books, from page to stage.

"A girl and I wrote a poem together in the car," I tell him, coming back from Columbus Day weekend. I looked at the road after getting out of Vermont and commented, 'It's a little darker and less spacious.' She said, 'That's the beginning of a poem.' I said, 'So what's the second line?' She thought for a moment then gave me a second line. It was bad. So I said, 'That's not the second line of this poem. The second line is, 'The stream rushed by the pumpkin.' 'You're right,' she said. Then she said, 'Tourists were eating the little towns.' 'You're getting the hang of it,' I told her, and we did the whole poem and called it 'Goethe's Line.'"

"Did you revise the poem?" Dad asks.

"No," I say. "She wanted to, but I told her I try never to rewrite. Like Shakespeare, never blot a line. Poetry should be like a fresco, the plaster is wet, and you paint it ala prima, on the first try. If it's bad, throw it away. You have only one chance."

"Now you're contradicting yourself," Dad says. "You're like the slam poets."
It's time for lunch. As usual we decide on going to the Pie Plate, and before the white, neoGreek house that he built almost sixty years ago and has lived in ever since, adding the white studio where he houses his five hundred paintings, meditations on the century; we admire the crisp November sunlight hitting the gray steps in front of the black door with its brass knocker in the shape of a Donatello hand. The cedar trees planted sixty years ago stand tall and sentinel the roundabout. The house is typical Dad, not grand, not a mansion, but not small, either — not a ranch, not a middle class home. It is just like in the Navy when he was neither an officer nor an enlisted man but a Chief Petty Officer. In-between. His edge in painting is an in-between edge too. He hobbles on his three Navy legs down the wooden steps and I say, "Why do you suppose some of the cedars have berries and some don't. Are they female?"
He says, "I believe they're androgynous."
He crunches with his limp painfully, slowly across the gray gravel, wobbling as he goes, and punches his radio garage opener at the old-fashioned heavy two-car garage door, which rattles hideously and grinds as it goes up, and he orders, in his boat captain way, "You stay here until I get the car out."
While I stand there as he crawls the old Cherokee jeep out, with the FUO 835 plates, I think about how he should put in a stair elevator before it is too late and of the visceral noises the old furnace gives off at night and ask him about it.

"It's the radiators," he says. "It doesn't mean anything. They're perfectly all right."

"Should you change the furnace?" I ask.

"I probably should," he concedes, "but I'll probably die first."

"How can you get it out?" I ask. "It won't go through the door."

He gives me his sly architect's glance. "In sections," he says. "It comes out in sections."

As a new homeowner, I think he's got it all figured out. He figured it out when he built the old

House in the Thirties, and when he dies, he's gotten so venerable in there himself, they'll probably have to take him out in sections, too.

"You know," I say. "These license plates drive me crazy. You think the letters must mean something, but they don't. Like yours: FUO 835."

"I know," he says. "They gave it to me. I didn't ask for it."

The Pie Plate is well past Avon on the road to Canton, on the left, and Dad drives so slowly that it takes forever to get there. He refuses to have an automatic shift so he has to pump the clutch every time with his bad foot, and it's a miracle that he's still on the road after ninety. He thinks it out all ahead of time, but shifts into fourth gear at fifteen miles an hour, so that the car shimmies and shakes, but every time someone beeps behind him he shouts, "Oh, shut up, goddamn you," and continues creeping along.

The Pie Plate is almost full when we get to the head of the line, and I say, "There is a table right there, Dad, for two," but he hangs doggedly back, pointing to the sign, "Wait for the hostess to seat you," even though he can't stand for long because if he does, he might topple over.

We sit down opposite each other as we have done a hundred times in the last years, and I say to him, "Did you ever notice that the ladies in here all have the same yellow hair? They've all been to the same hairdresser's."

"It's probably meant to be that way," he says. "It's Sunday."

The waitress comes up and smiles. Her name is Barbara. "How are we doing today?" She asks. And dad looks at me and says, "Do we already know what we want?"

"A deluxe hamburger and chicken soup," I say.

"And you, sir?" she asks him.

"The same," he says. The waitress starts to back away, but Dad is too quick for her. "Oh," he says, "could ...could you bring me the check?" He hates to wait at the end of the meal for the check, so, very politely, in his best schoolboy manners, he asks for the check at the beginning of the meal, as if he were asking for something naughty."

We put the menus away and wait. Everybody is old in this place, and I think Betty Friedan, with the FOUNTAIN OF AGE was really onto something.

I say to Dad, "Do you know something about Charity?" Charity is not the religious thing but the name of my sister. And he says, "No, what?" And I say, "Well, you know Prudence, her older sister, as she gets older gets more like Prudence. But you know what? Charity is getting more like Prudence, too."

"Charity is more intelligent than Prudence," he says. "Always has been."

"Family resemblance's grow on people as they get older," Dad says, which I have never thought about.

Dad is silent. He doesn't like to talk openly about people. He doesn't like my saying it all, hanging it all out, but, Jesus, Dad may live to be a hundred and ten years old and outlast me; why not let a little of it hang out now before we're all gone?"

"It's like Sue and me," he says. "Betty Friedan says the trouble with men and women is that their lives are different; things don't fit. Women's lives are compartmentalized. First they're little girls, then they get to be sex objects, then they are mothers, then comes the empty nest. Just about the time the man is getting tired of his career, the woman wants to go out and work. That's what happened to Sue. She was on the Hartford Symphony, the hospital, the Wadsworth Atheneum, and the Volunteer Nurses, running around like a committee woman just what at fifty-eight, pretty early, I was retiring to paint. My partner, and I, at the architectural office, looked around and decided that all the people we knew had already built their houses and that the young people wanted somebody younger for their homes, so we would get fewer and fewer jobs. We both had independent incomes so we shut the office down. He went into gardening in a big way and I began to paint. Well it made Sue mad because she didn't think I was doing my duty."

I shrug. "A woman told me to never let the woman get control or all is lost."

Dad looks sort of forlornly at me, a little tired, and says, "I always thought the opposite. Shucks. Let them have control." Then under his shaggy eyebrows, with his thinned hair wisping in the air, he adds, "At least let them think so." He laughs at his own joke. It is a good one on Betty Friedan.

He is looking a little bleary eyed, though, even though I've never seen him cry, so to change the subject I say USA Today's top story is that gifted children find U.S. schools boring.

"Well," he says ruefully, "you were always a bright child. But I knew by the time I got to Yale that I was in the middle of the class. But you're right. It's not news. Heck. I was that way too. I used to like to cut it up in class."

"Why did you do that? Were you bored — or just gifted?"

"Partly because I wasn't as fast as the other students. I knew I couldn't get the top grades."

We munch our hamburgers and sip ice water. It is always this way. The girl doesn't bring the check until the end and says, "You're sure you don't want desert?" But both of us are trying to keep our figures. He weighs twenty pounds less than I do now. I almost weigh as much as he did when he got out of the Navy in 1945 and came home to strap me with the razor blade strap, forced me to shoot the Colt 45 that I could barely hold at arms length, and nearly blasted my eardrums in, like a giant rose up and threw over the dining room table on us children, told me I would never be as good as my brother, and warned me that if I didn't shape up I would be the black sheep of the family. He wanted me to be a soldier. It was 1945. I was eleven. A man changes; a boy changes, too.

I look at him across the table and think of my recent nightmare. It isn't

the Colt 45. He gave me that and his .32 to the Avon police a few years
ago, thank God, No, I am visiting suddenly in his empty surrealist twelve-
room, three-bathroom house, sleeping in my sister's bed, with her children's
books and the dresser, with the yellow striped, stuffed leopard with the
shining green dadaist eyes, and Dad and I are alone in the house; it is past
midnight, three o'clock in the morning and he calls. It's his heart, he says.
He wants me to give him an injection.
What if I don't? What if I call the doctor? We have been talking about
Dr. Kevorkian that day, the suicide doctor, "Doctor Death." And Dad has
said, "He's interesting. But is he insane?"
Well, I think, if I don't give him the injection, what if he dies, and it is my
fault? I shudder. So I give him the injection, but I think, what if he has set
me up? What if it is lethal? What if it's one of his surrealist jokes? The
real doctor comes and sees the syringe. He puts it in his black valise. They
check it out. They find it was lethal. Dad is dead. They have me. They
say I did it for the money.
It is dangerous to sleep in your father's house.
He knows nothing of my nightmare. It would probably amuse him, if he
could paint a picture of it. But I can't tell him the nightmare. So he
shuffles to the cash register. I look back on the last sixty years, and I know,
for a fact, I owe him. Yet he still pays. What are the two most important
books in the world? Ho ho. Mother's cookbook and Dad's checkbook. I
learned that one from my father-in-law. He got it, I think, from Mark
Twain.
In the parking lot dad sticks out his hand. He has to slip the cane over to

his left arm to do it. He loops the crook of the cane over the sleeve and says, "Well, I'll be seein' ya."

He says "ya" not "you". It's his Groton accent. His Yale best. Just the way he says "ruf" not "roof". It's the little things. He looks like Grandmother Betty, his mother. You'd never know he was Walter's son. Walter was about five feet eight; Dad is six three, and he hasn't shrunk that much. It's only that he tells his doctor, "I'm scared to stand up". Why?" The doctor asks. "Because I'm scared if I do, I'll fall over."

His big, bony hand is still rough from pulling the halyard and holding the main sheet of his catboat, which even last year he sailed overnight to Fisher's Island, taking with him French wine in a can — that amuses him, that the French got wine into a can — and a copy of PILGRIM'S PROGRESS. Anchored out there, he read it by flashlight.

Finally, this summer, he gave the catboat away to the Mystic Seaport. Now, this coming Spring, he plans to buy an eleven-foot Maine rowboat with lug sail and put his two-and-a-half horsepower Japanese cruise-and-carry outboard on the thing and raise and lower the mast to get to sea from the lagoon inside the New York, New Haven, and Hartford rail bridge. He figures if he can't walk, he might as well still sail.

Just recently, he says, he started cutting the pages in Grandfather's old leather-bound edition of Shakespeare and has read all of Henry IV, Macbeth, Hamlet, A Midsummer Night's Dream, and The Tempest.

"I do it in bed, cutting open the pages one by one because I like to even

though it ruins the antiquarian value of the books. It's a nice edition.
Shakespeare. It's like touching first base, you know."
"Well, I'll be seein' ya," he says again.
Will you? It's the same every time now. I never know if I'll see him again;
I never know if he'll be laid out when I get there. I never know whether it
will be his last joke. I never know if I'll still be here. An appointment with
your father — as if it were some euphemism for judgement and death.
He is still standing by his car fumbling at the door when I drive by on my
way out. I toot twice, and he gives me the paternal wave; I can remember
it from when he used to put me on the Pullman to New York more than
fifty years ago to send me back to my mother's after a paternal visit. What
I didn't know then, I know now.
His rumpled clothes hang on him like a scarecrow. He hasn't bought a
new thread of clothes in twenty-five years. That's how long he has been
painting too. Five hundred pictures. And today he started a new one. It
was called "The Unsolicited Invasion".
Vita brevis, Ars longa est, they used to say. Well, in this case, the art was
the short end of the stick and the life was long. There he stands, shaking
out his last salute. An American Original. An American Master. I turn
and don't look back. As I said, I owe him.
We'll miss him.

Program Notes from Paris

The USA may be considered the generator of a mechanistic culture, but certain signs, including the painting of Sage Goodwin, indicate another side of this point of view. Surely one cannot live outside the culture but, particularly in the United States, one can express opinion, not always flattering — see Goodwin's MOTORING NOSTALGIA and other images, and the new cars in the cemetery in PLANNED OBSOLESCENCE, the diabolical smile of the salesman in ASK YOUR SALESMAN, and the marketing director who is "the maker of anxiety". As to escapism, Goodwin depicts this in THE DIONYSIACS where white and black mix their frenetic dances, in WAR AND PEACE, where the guitarist is a militant. See also BIG LEAGUES, the innocent young person is caught in the professional baseball world, and THE OLD SOLDIERS, the SPIRIT OF 1876, and THE FOUNDER — all ironic allegories, put-ons of patriotic cliches, and satires of business.

The violence of these denials leads naturally to dream, symbols, and poetry. I don't need to describe other canvasses showing the same strangenesses such as GRAND LINE NOWHERE, THE DANCE LESSON, RESPONSIBLE DREAM, and MAGIC ECHO — one of the images that show most clearly the latent influence of surrealism. I like particularly THE EMPTY STATION and its echo of de Chirico.

Goodwin cannot refuse reality because his means of expression are realistic and the violence always surfaces of the search for a second reality, a symbolic and ironic reality. In the succession of canvasses, I see a magic very different from the seductions of the naifs. Naif painting reproduces things, landscapes and portraits, as if made by a child, with the same purity and maladroitness. But Goodwin is an adult painting allegories not without a relevant dexterity which one might even call American Expressionism. Goodwin combats the omnipresent publicity, for example, and the comics of his country with their very own weapons, or takes arms against the images of science fiction; this graphics without equivocation cannot help but capture effectively the motions of its primitive heroes. Within its limits it's a very authentic art, and I would go so far as to say that in its specificity of style and originality it is much fresher than the schools of American painting borrowed from European design and re-exported under ephemeral names, such as action painting, or pop art where little playthings more or less become fads in the studios. Instead Goodwin introduces a style based on revolt and poetry that has never been shown in Paris. It has nothing to do with pop art, as certain New York critics have tried superficially to imply — pop was a deracinated dadaism, which certainly Goodwin's paintings are not.

Right: these pictures are not "la peinture!" They say, "they are badly painted," or, "You are not a painter." Let me tell you as Frenchman and critic of the new wave that in this domain Goodwin is a right good companion along with the surrealists and their precursors and with all the painters of literary works — and yes, even, with the naifs.

To that lady who said at one of Goodwin's exhibitions she had never seen such a horrible picture, I would tell her: you say this and yet you hang a bloody crucifix over your head. Give me a break.

Marcel Jean / Paris/ 1968

ONE MAN SHOWS

1964 Ahda Artzt Gallery, 142 West 57th Street, New York, New York.

1966 Ahda Artzt Gallery, 142 West 57th Street, New York, New York.

1968 Galerie Mona Lisa, Rue du Bac at Boulevard Raspail, Paris, France.

1970 Austin Arts Center, Trinity College, Hartford, Connecticut.

1977 Avon Library, Avon, Connecticut, friends of the Avon Library.

1983 New Britain Art Museum, New Britain, Connecticut.

1985 Joseloff Gallery, University of Hartford, Hartford, Connecticut, A RETROSPECTIVE.

1989 Goodspeed Opera House, HENRY SAGE GOODWIN, A TRIBUTE, May 23-June 25, 1989.

GROUP SHOWS

1973 Seventeenth Regional Juried Show, Mystic Art Association, July 21-Aug. 17, 1973, Mystic Art Association, Robert Cale, Juror, WARD HUBBARD PRIZE for MEMORY OF ATLANTIC CITY.

1974 Mystic Art Invitational, Mystic Art Association, Mystic, Connecticut.

1974 Stonington Art Gallery Invitational.

Other group jury shows at the Canton, Connecticut, Art association, in Farmington, Hartford, New York, Maine and Massachusetts.

BIBLIOGRAPHY

Avon News, June 8, 1989; "Henry Sage Goodwin's Paintings on Exhibit," p.17

Berkman, Florence, The Middletown Press, Jan. 11, 1985, Lively Arts, p.3; "Art: Works by Sage Goodwin at Hartford Art School." Review.

Batz, Harry, The Hartford Courant, "Pointing Invigorates Retired architect," Friday, Jan. 9, 1971.

Cox-Chapman, Molly, NORTHEAST, The Hartford Courant, May 28, 1989, cover article, "Sage Goodwin, and the Art of the Misfit," cover photo by Jim Meehan, p.8.

Curren, Elizabeth G., New Haven Register, June 4, 1989, p. 5, "Hanging at the Goodspeed."

The Hartford Courant, "New Alliance Trend in Arts, Speaker Says", Friday, June 16, 1972, p. 60.

Hanson, Bernard, The Hartford Courant, "Goodwin's Clear Bold Viewpoints", Sunday, Jan. 6, 1984, p. G6.

The Hartford Times, Hartford, Connecticut, Dec. 2, 1969, "Architect Turned Painter to Show works;" cut of Haunted Temple in South America on exhibit at Avon Library.

Jean, Marcel, "Not Quite Cricket," program notes, Galerie Mona Lisa, Paris, 1968.

Josten, Henry E., The Pictorial Gazette, Hartford, Connecticut, "Artist Goodwin Honored," May 30, 1989.

Mahoney, Michael, Chairman Trinity College Department of Fine Arts, Hartford, Connecticut, 1970, program notes, with Dean Walker, Bonita Coriale, Deborah Endersby, Louise Riskin, Bruce Foxley, Craig Greaver, William Richards.

McMahon, Charlene, Review of FUTURE'S FRIENDS, The Farmington Valley Post, Nov. 1, 1999, Vol. 10, No.12.

Miller-Keller, Andrea, Curator of Contemporary Art, Wadsworth Atheneum, Hartford, Connecticut, program notes to Henry Sage Goodwin/A Tribute, Goodspeed Opera House, 1989.

Park East, Serving the Silk Stocking District, New York, Morton B. Lawrence editor/publisher, Vol 3. No 40, photo cut of IT'S MY MAN.

Roberts, Collette, FRANCE-AMERIQUE, Le Courrier des Etats-Unis, Le Courier des Arts, Review of show at Ahda Artzt, 20 Oct., 1966, Serie C.F. No 710.

Sabatini, Josh, Valley News, Oct. 14, 1999, "Ninety year Old Resident Author Keeps Busy with New Book," p.3.

Wardell, Edward R., Yale Alumni Review, '27, p.97, item from Alf Bingham, author of THE TIFFANY FORTUNE (Abeel and Leet, 1995).

Whitbeck, Doris, The Hartford Courant, Sunday, Dec. 30, 1989, "Goodwin Retrospective to Open", p. G.9.